In the Beginning The Creation

by Steven J. Wallace

© 2018 One Stone Press.
All rights reserved. No part of this book may be reproduced in any form without written permission of the publisher.

Published by:
One Stone Press
979 Lovers Lane
Bowling Green, KY 42103

Printed in the United States of America

ISBN-13: 978-1-941422-28-1

Teacher Manual Available

979 Lovers Lane Ste. 1
Bowling Green, KY 42103
1-800-428-0121 • www.onestone.com

Table of Contents

1. In the Beginning — Genesis, a Foundation 5
2. In the Beginning — The Creation 13
3. In the Beginning — The Family 21
4. In the Beginning — Satan's Allurement 29
5. In the Beginning — Sin and Its Consequences 39
6. In the Beginning — Sin and Its Corruption of Worship, Brotherly Love, and the Family — Genesis 4 47
7. In the Beginning — Sin and Its Epitaph 55
8. In the Beginning — Sin and Its Epitaph 65
9. In the Beginning — Sin's End: Judgment 75
10. In the Beginning — Noah's Deliverance 83
11. In the Beginning — Life in the New World 91
12. In the Beginning — The Beginning of Languages and Nation Formation 99
13. In the Beginning — The Beginning of the Scheme of Redemption 107

In the Beginning — Genesis, a Foundation

Lesson 1

The book of Genesis is about *beginnings*. A beginning is a point in which something starts. Genesis means *beginning*. This book begins the Holy Scriptures and shows us the beginning of very important things. It serves as a foundation for all the Scriptures which follow. Do you know what a foundation is? A *foundation* is the basis or support for something. It could be an idea or fact which serves as a foundation for a belief or teaching. For example, being friendly is a foundation for having friends. An unfriendly person will likely not have friends (Prov. 18:24).

We may be more familiar with the example of a house. The beginning of a house is its foundation. Every house needs a good foundation, and the house can only be as strong as the foundation it is built upon. The *structure* of the house rests upon a *foundation*. Jesus drew a picture in our minds of two men in Luke 6:48, 49. The one who faithfully hears and obeys is as "...a man building a house, who dug deep and laid the foundation on the rock." This man's house survived in the storm. The other man was one who heard but did not obey,

Key Passage

"In the beginning God created the heavens and the earth."

(Gen. 1:1)

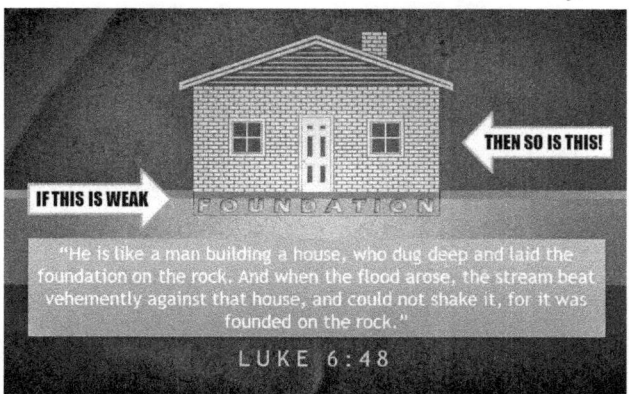

"If the foundations are destroyed, What can the righteous do?" (Psalm 11:3)

Paul draws a parallel that ties Jesus to Adam by quoting from Genesis 2:7, "And so it is written, 'The first man Adam became a living being.' The last Adam became a life-giving spirit."

(1 Cor. 15:45)

The "first" and "last" Adam stand and fall together. One cannot be fiction and the other a fact.

and his house fell in the storm because his house was "without a foundation." Without a deep and stable foundation, any house is easily destroyed.

Like a foundation to a house, Genesis is the foundation to the Bible. Much of the teaching in the rest of the Bible is anchored in Genesis. It is not surprising, therefore, that every New Testament writer refers to things rooted in Genesis. The first eleven chapters of Genesis have been viciously attacked by unbelievers and compromisers. Some dismiss this portion of Holy Scripture as unimportant. However, we should consider the warning of Psalm 11:3.

The New Testament writers viewed Genesis as true history, and nearly every New Testament book has a reference that goes back to Genesis. There are over 100 passages in the New Testament that reference Genesis! We would not have a clear understanding of sin without the teaching of Genesis 3–11. We should also appreciate that Jesus agreed with the Genesis account

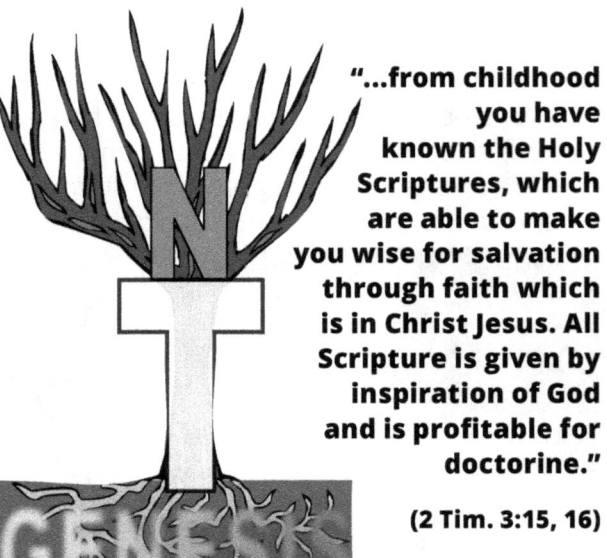

"...from childhood you have known the Holy Scriptures, which are able to make you wise for salvation through faith which is in Christ Jesus. All Scripture is given by inspiration of God and is profitable for doctorine."

(2 Tim. 3:15, 16)

LESSON 1 In the Beginning — Genesis, a Foundation

of creation, the first couple, the flood, and of the destruction of Sodom and Gomorrah (Mk. 10:6; Matt. 24:37–39; 10:15; etc.).

Likewise, the apostles agreed with Genesis. They affirmed that death entered through Adam's sin, that Eve was deceived, that the serpent was real, etc. (1 Cor. 15:21, 22; 1 Tim. 2:13, 14; 2 Cor. 11:3; 2 Pet. 2:5–7; etc.). Much more could be stated of the connection between Genesis and the New Testament, but picture Genesis like the roots of a tree and the New Testament as the actual tree. The tree is only as good as the root. If an ax is laid to the root of the tree, the tree itself will die. When people attack Genesis, they are actually undermining the rest of the Bible.

1. 1 Corinthians 15:21, 22, "For since by _____ came death, by _____ also came the resurrection of the dead. For as in _____ all die, even so in _____ all shall be made alive."

QUESTIONS:

2. What does the word Genesis mean? _____
   _____

3. What is the purpose of a foundation? _____
   _____
   _____

4. How complete would the Bible be without Genesis? _____
   _____

5. How connected is Genesis to the New Testament? Identify some of these connections. _____
   _____
   _____

6. Why is this connection important? _____
   _____
   _____

The Value of Genesis

Because Genesis addresses beginnings, it is very helpful to us. Here are some ways Genesis benefits us.

Genesis helps us understand God's word. In speaking of the Old Testament Scriptures, Paul told Timothy, "and that from childhood you have known the Holy Scriptures, which are able to make you wise for salvation through faith which is in Christ Jesus" (2 Tim. 3:15). These Scriptures make one wise for salvation through faith. In the very next sentence, Paul stated, "All Scripture is given by inspiration of God, and is profitable for doctrine..." (2 Tim. 3:16). Likewise, the Lord said in John 5:46, 47, "For if you believed Moses, you would believe Me; for he wrote about Me. But if you do not believe his writings, how will you believe My words?" Moses wrote about Jesus in Genesis. Jesus is the seed of woman, who would crush the serpent's head (Gen. 3:15). Jesus is the seed of Abraham, by which all the families of the earth would be blessed (Gen. 22:18; Gal. 3:16). Jesus is the fulfillment of what Jacob spoke of the tribe of Judah in Genesis 49:8-12. Genesis and Jesus are forever tied together!

Genesis helps us understand God's world. We learn from Genesis why so much violence, conflict, confusion, suffering, and death exist in our world. Genesis shows our world is cursed with the consequences of sin (Gen. 3:15-19). Genesis provides a key to explain why fossilized remains exist in the earth's crust, why so many languages exist in the world today, why there are wild and ravenous beasts, and even why there are prickly thorns and thistles.

Genesis helps us understand the meaning of very important things. Because the meaning of anything is tied to its beginning, Genesis helps us understand the significance of life, marriage, death, and even the reason for wearing clothing.

Genesis helps us understand our adversary—Satan! It identifies him as cunning and crafty in his attack on God's word. Genesis shows that Satan seeks to deceive man by appealing to man's pride and desires. Paul tells us to learn from this: "But I fear, lest somehow, as the serpent deceived Eve by his craftiness, so your minds may be corrupted from the simplicity that is in Christ" (2 Cor. 11:3).

QUESTIONS:

7. Who wrote Genesis?_____

LESSON 1 In the Beginning — Genesis, a Foundation

8. Did Jesus say it is okay to believe His words and reject what Moses wrote? _____

9. Name some things in Genesis which are about Jesus. _____
   _____

10. Name four ways Genesis helps us today. _____
    _____
    _____
    _____

Genesis 1:1

"In the beginning God created the heavens and the earth."

We can gain so much information from the very first verse of the Bible. This verse is our key passage and is the key to believing all the truth taught in the Bible. Let us observe some important lessons.

"In the beginning" is a phrase that speaks of *time*. This passage teaches that time as we know it had a beginning. It is one of the dimensions or parts of our universe. We refer to time in three ways (past, present, and future). We measure time in various ways such as seconds, minutes, hours, days, weeks, months, and years.

"God" is shown here to have existed *before* time. God did not begin in time, but time as we know it, began with God. Genesis chapter one does not teach the beginning of God, but the beginning of time, space, and matter. The Hebrew word for *God* is *Elohim* and suggests a plurality of persons. We later learn that our God is made up of three distinct, divine Persons. There is the Father, Son, and Holy Spirit. All three were at work in the creation, and all three existed before time. As the Son, Jesus followed the Father's will in creating the universe (Heb. 1:1, 2). The Holy Spirit is also God and is seen in the creation as hovering over the face of the deep (Gen. 1:2).

11. John 17:5, "And now, O _____, glorify Me together with Yourself, with the glory which _____ had with You _____ the _____ was."

> "God, who at various times and in various ways spoke in time past to the fathers by the prophets, has in these last days spoken to us by His Son, whom He has appointed heir of all things, through whom also He made the worlds."
>
> (Heb. 1:1, 2)

12. Hebrews 1:8, 9, "But to the _____ He says: 'Your throne, O _____, is forever and ever; A scepter of righteousness is the scepter of Your Kingdom. You have loved righteousness and hated lawlessness; Therefore _____, Your _____, has anointed You with the oil of gladness more than Your companions.'"

13. John 20:17, "Jesus said to her, 'Do not cling to Me, for I have not yet ascended to My _____; but go to My brethren and say to them, 'I am _____ to My _____ and your _____, and to My _____ and your _____.'"

"Created" tells us of the energy and power of God. God took something which did not exist and made it exist. This Hebrew word is found three times in Genesis 1 and signifies the creation of something new from nothing each time. Creation was not a product of chance and random natural explosions, but rather of supernatural intelligence.

"The heavens" speaks of space. Space is another dimension or part of our universe, and it, like time, is viewed in three different ways. We observe space by height, depth, and width.

"The earth" speaks of matter. Everything around us and even our bodies are made up of matter. We *commonly* observe matter as a solid, a liquid, or as a gas. What is matter made of? Matter is made up of very small particles called *atoms*, which scientists

LESSON 1 In the Beginning — Genesis, a Foundation

tell us are made up of protons, neutrons, and electrons. Atoms are in fact so small that we cannot see them even with the strongest microscopes. No one has seen an atom, and yet nearly everyone believes they exist because there is evidence that they do, even as we believe that God exists based on evidence. Also appreciate the power that is in matter. You can burn wood and get a lot of heat from it. However, scientists have found that the splitting of atoms (called fission) produces large amounts of energy (such as is seen in an atomic bomb). Such power should testify to us of the great power of the Creator of the atom. He upholds all things by the word of His *power* and has the power to *dissolve* and *melt* every element in the universe (Heb. 1:1–3; 2 Pet. 3:10, 11). Our God is an awesome God!

It is important for us to appreciate the greatness of the Creator over the created. Because of His excellent state, we find the answer as to how and why the universe is here. Scientists tell us the universe had a beginning; the Bible tells us that Jesus began the creation. We don't have to ask, "Where did God come from?" Because He is outside of time, space, and matter, He needs no beginning. Notice how God surpasses these dimensions:

Time

God is greater than time because He created time. Therefore, He cannot be measured by time. Peter stated, "But, beloved, do not forget this one thing, that with the Lord one day is as a thousand years, and a thousand years as one day" (2 Pet. 3:8; see Job 36:26).

Space

God is greater than space because He created space. This shows us that God could know what goes on in all of space since He is over it all.

14. Explain: "'Can anyone hide himself in secret places, So I shall not see him?' says the LORD; 'Do I not fill heaven and earth?' says the LORD'" (Jer. 23:24). _____

_____

_____

_____

_____

_____

_____

12   In the Beginning — The Creation

Matter

15. Explain: God is greater than matter because He created matter. His excellence over matter is seen in the fact that He is Spirit and therefore cannot dwell in physical temples (Jn. 4:24; Acts 17:24). _____

_____

_____

Genesis gives the answer to the riddle "How did the universe and all that is in it come into existence?" Asking, "Who created God" would be as silly as asking, "Who created the Creator?" The Creator does not need to be created. Only things with a beginning had a cause. Your life was caused to come into this world. However, God had no beginning, and therefore He has no "birthday." Nothing started without God. He has always existed, and that is what makes Him God.

QUESTIONS:

16. Does Genesis teach that God had a beginning or that the universe had a beginning? _____

_____

17. What are the three Persons that make up God? _____

_____

18. Did Jesus exist before the creation? Scripture: _____

_____

19. How do we know that God does not need a beginning or starting point?

_____

20. When a man lied to the Holy Spirit in Acts 5:1-4, to whom did Peter say he lied? See Acts 5:4. _____

_____

_____

Lesson 2

In the Beginning — The Creation

Genesis provides us with a concise record of the creation and asserts that all things were brought into existence within a brief period of time, six days. Genesis claimed *a beginning* when man once claimed, "There was no beginning." Until recently, it was a mainstream belief of the scientific community that matter was in a *steady state* and *always* existed. Eventually, science caught up with the Bible and now affirms that there was *a beginning*. Let us learn that God's word is always true while man's word is often in a steady state of change. What is believed by man today is often revised or rejected tomorrow.

Skeptics continue to deny that there was an intelligent power to govern and complete the creation. In rejecting the answer "There is a God!", they are left to believe that the creation created itself! Their faith without God as Creator is as foolish as believing a massive airplane could be produced in full working order from a tornado that tore through a junkyard! Who would believe such? Without God, atheists force themselves to believe that from *absolute nothingness* came *something*! From that moment where *nothing* gave birth to *something,* a series of cosmic disturbances with billions of years of mistakes resulted in the creation of life and our present orderly universe. Have you ever observed something come forth from nothing? Even in a good magic trick, it only *appears* to happen, and you still have the magician and the tools he uses (such as a rabbit coming out of a hat). You never see absolute nothingness produce anything. Science observes that everything that *begins* to exist has been caused

Key Passage

"Let all the earth fear the LORD; Let all the inhabitants of the world stand in awe of Him. For He spoke, and it was done; He commanded, and it stood fast."

(Psalm 33:8, 9)

to exist. For life and intelligence to begin to exist, such must have been caused by an intelligent and living source.

The First Week of Time—Seven Days!

The very first week of time consisted of seven days. There were six days in which God worked and one day of rest. This first week is fundamental to our understanding of the universe and our place in it.

DAY ONE: LIGHT

Read Genesis 1:3–5. It is important to see that this light existed before the sun was created. Without light, life would cease to exist; however, Genesis teaches us that God is the author of light and our life is dependent upon Him, not the sun. Later, light is seen spiritually as representing knowledge and righteousness. Darkness stands as an emblem of evil (Jn. 1:6–11; 3:19; Eph. 5:8). There is no darkness in God (1 Jn. 1:5). Jesus dwells in unapproachable light (1 Tim. 6:16; Ps. 104:2). This light is so powerful that man cannot stand in it. We find glimpses of its power in the New Testament (Matt. 17:1ff; Acts 26:13; Rev. 1:16). Spiritually, Jesus came to earth to bring forth light in the knowledge of God (2 Cor. 4:4–6). Preaching the gospel brings the light of God's truth to a sinfully dark world. It was on the first day of the week, on the Day of Pentecost, that the first gospel sermon was preached (Acts 2:1ff).

FILL IN THE BLANK:

1. 1 John 1:5, "This is the _____ which we have heard from Him and declare to you, that _____ is _____ and in Him is no _____ at all."

NOTE TO STUDENT:

Carefully read the Scriptures that are cited below for each day of creation.

DAY TWO: DIVISION OF WATER

Read Genesis 1:6–8. The earth was previously without form and void, or "empty" (Gen. 1:2). Here, God took the water and divided it with an expanse of space which He calls "heaven." The effect of this resulted in two reservoirs of water—water above and water below the sky.

DAY THREE: DRY LAND, GRASS, HERBS, FRUIT TREES

Read Genesis 1:9–13. God made the waters "under the heavens" gather together to form seas, which also made dry land appear. The earth was made to bring forth all kinds of vegetarian life. Each of these was created to produce a seed which would then bring about the specific kind of plant. This is exactly what has been observed down through time. The Law of Biogenesis is a scientific law that asserts living material can only come from living material. All living things produce living things within their specific and genetic *kind*. This scientific law stands as a contradiction to evolution but is in complete agreement with the Holy Scripture. A fruit tree yields fruit with a seed, which reproduces the same particular kind of tree. Have you ever seen an apple seed grow into an orange tree? Significantly, Genesis teaches these forms of life were made before the sun existed. The point: Life is dependent upon the living God, not the sun!

DAY FOUR: SUN, MOON, AND STARS

Read Genesis 1:14–19. The emphasis of these created bodies was to provide light to the earth. We see that the earth is the centerpiece of God's creation. God did not create the sun first, as evolutionists would have us believe. According to the Bible, the earth is actually older than the sun. Will you believe God's word or man's word?

DAY FIVE: SEA CREATURES AND BIRDS

Read Genesis 1:20–23. God saw fit to decorate the seas and the heavens with all kinds of various forms of life. These creatures were created suitable for these domains and fully capable of reproducing. Yet, each one was also set within a fixed kind. This is what we still observe today. Have you ever seen a fish give birth to a bird?

DAY SIX: LAND ANIMALS AND MANKIND

Read Genesis 1:24–31. Like day five, these creatures were created to reproduce after their kind. We also find the high point of God's creation which came after the animals were created: He created mankind, as male and female (see Gen. 5:1, 2). Man is not an animal but a separate kind, designed to be ruler over the creation. No animal rules over the creation, but mankind does. Because man is made in the image of God, he is different from all other life forms on earth. Unlike animals, man possesses abilities to formulate ideas and concepts, to reason, to debate, to appreciate, to love, and to hate. He has spiritual qualities and searches for truth and the purpose of life. The end of the Bible teaches exactly what the beginning of the Bible implies. Because God is Creator of man and man is created as the offspring of God, we are to honor and worship Him (Acts 17:24–31).

DAY SEVEN: REST

Read Genesis 2:1–3. God rested on the seventh day because man is created to rest. Jesus even called His disciples to come and rest a while (Mk. 6:31). With this day of rest, we were given the basis for our seven day week. There is nothing observed in nature which constitutes a seven day week. A day is based on one spinning rotation of the earth. A year is based on one orbital revolution of the earth around the sun. But our seven day week is based on the creation of the universe!

The book of Hebrews shows that there is still a rest that awaits the people of God, and so the seventh-day rest was symbolic for a time which yet awaits us in heaven (Heb. 4:1–10). Yet, we must be diligent to obey God in order to inherit it. "Let us therefore be diligent to enter that rest, lest anyone fall according to the same example of disobedience" (Heb. 4:11).

QUESTIONS:

2. What is the "rest" that we wait for? _____

3. How do we attain this rest? _____
   _____

4. Without the answer, "There is a God!", how could we explain the existence of life? _____
   _____

5. Did God need to be created?_____
   _____

6. What does the Law of Biogenesis teach? _____
   _____

7. Is it reasonable to believe that something can "pop up" out of absolutely nothing? If it is, give an example. If not, explain. _____

8. What is older, grass or the sun? Explain why. _____

9. Can fish give birth to birds? Why or why not? _____

10. Is man a complex animal? Support your answer. _____

Who is a Bible Atheist?

Not everyone believes what the Bible says about creation. Atheists deny God and His word. It is important to know who the Bible identifies as an atheist. Atheism is weakly defined today by some as "the lack of belief in a god." This definition is too broad and would require that anything which cannot believe is to be considered an atheist. Are babies, stones, serpents, and scorpions atheists because they do not possess a belief in God? That is absurd! Traditionally, atheism has been defined as the denial of the existence of God. An atheist can believe, but chooses to deny the existence of God. Psalm 14:1 tells us that the fool says, "There is no God." John charges such a position as making God a liar (I Jn. 5:10).

A Bible atheist denies the existence of God and is identified as a "fool," or senseless person (Ps. 14:1).

One may also be an atheist by suppressing God in his mind. To "suppress" is to hold something down. He takes the thought of "a God" and holds it down so that he doesn't have to think about God. Psalm 10:4 describes such a one: "The wicked in his proud countenance does not seek God; God is in none of his thoughts." Because God is in none of his thoughts, he is not moved or influenced by God's will. One is simply an atheist whether he claims to be or not.

Another form of an atheist is one who willfully forgets God. For some, great materialistic wealth has made them blind to God.

FILL IN THE BLANK:

11. Proverbs 30:8, 9, "Remove falsehood and lies far from me; Give me neither _____ nor _____—Feed me with the food allotted to me; Lest I be full and _____ You, And say, 'Who is the LORD?' Or lest I be _____ and steal, And _____ the name of my God."

Finally, another form of atheism is to deny the word of God. One may actually profess to "know God" and yet deny Him (Titus 1:15, 16; Matt. 7:21-23). Our relationship to Jesus is based upon His word which is the Father's word (Jn. 12:48, 49). When we deny His word, we are actually rejecting God.

All in all, atheists are those with "...no hope and without God in the world" (Eph. 2:12). As believers and disciples of Christ, we cannot reject the book of Genesis. In the next lesson, we will look at those who reject the days of Genesis as literal days and some theories that they have created which deny the word of God. Let us appreciate that the Genesis acccount of creation shows us that the beginning of creation was "very good" (Gen. 1:31). It shows us that creation is the product of an all-powerful God, that order comes from intelligence, and that things exist by the word of His power. It shows us that mankind was created superior to animals and has a place in creation as the *offspring* of God. You were made special and are to honor God with your life.

> "The fool has said in his heart, 'There is no God.' They are corrupt, They have done abominable works, There is none who does good."
>
> (Ps. 14:1)

LESSON 2 In the Beginning — The Creation

QUESTIONS:

12. Is it foolish to reject God (Ps. 14:1)? _____
_____
_____

13. Why do wicked people not seek God (Ps. 10:4?_____
_____
_____

14. Can someone claim to "know God" and yet deny Him (Titus 1:15, 16)? ___
_____
_____

15. Can a person be saved as an atheist (Eph. 2:12)?_____
_____
_____

16. Can people reject God's word and be saved? _____
_____
_____

17. What are some ways you have seen people reject God's word in the Bible?_____
_____
_____
_____
_____
_____
_____

In the Beginning — The Family

To understand the meaning and the makeup of the family, we must look at the origin of the family. Remember from the first lesson that Genesis is a book of beginnings and that we understand the meaning of anything by looking at its origin. Genesis 1:26–2:25 gives us a lot of information that is related to our understanding of the family. Before we look at the family, have you ever asked, "Why does only mankind enter into marriage?"

Mankind—The Image Bearer

If God did not design man and woman in the image of God, they would not be able to marry. That may sound a little strange at first, but when you consider how man is different from the animal world, then marriage only makes sense for descendants of Adam and Eve. Man was the last of all the great kinds of creatures God made. In Genesis 1:25 we read, "And God made the beast of the earth according to its kind, cattle according to its kind, and everything that creeps on the earth according to its kind. And God saw that it was good." Though "good" and made on day six, why do land animals not marry? Have you ever seen two animals enter inter a marriage?

Three areas where man differs from animals

Mankind was created in the likeness of God. Man and woman were created as a three-part masterpiece, unique from any other creature God made.

Key Passage

"And the LORD God said, 'It is not good that man should be alone; I will make him a helper comparable to him'."

(Gen. 2:18)

"So God created man in His own image; in the image of God He created him; male and female He created them."

(Gen. 1:27)

Mankind was made of earth. His body was made from earthly elements (Gen. 2:7). King David wrote in Psalm 103:14, "For He knows our frame; He remembers that we are dust." His son Solomon also penned, "...all are from the dust, and all return to dust" (Eccl. 3:20). Man would not be able to marry if he did not have a body. At the same time, trees came from the earth, but trees do not marry (Gen. 1:11).

Man was made living. God made man not to come forth from the earth and stay in one place as a tree, but He made him animated clay. Man breathes and moves. God "breathed into his nostrils... and man became a living being" (Gen. 2:7). Paul preached that God gives to all life and breath (Acts 17:25). Man would not be able to marry if he did not have the breath of life. However, even animals have such but do not marry (Gen. 7:15).

Man was made with a spirit. While man shares the first two qualities with animals, man is unique in that he has a spirit. God is Spirit, and He created man with a spirit (Jn. 4:24). Zechariah wrote that God "forms the spirit of man within him" (Zech. 12:1). God is the Father of spirits (Heb. 12:9.) Solomon expressed that the spirit returns to God who gave it (Eccl. 12:7). He also revealed man's accountability: "Let us hear the conclusion of the whole matter: Fear God and keep His commandments, For this is man's all. For God will bring every work into judgment, Including every secret thing, Whether good or evil" (Eccl. 12:13, 14). Because man is made in the image of God, he is an intelligent and moral creature who can know *good and evil*. Therefore, man, unlike the animals, is accountable for his decision making while alive in the body. Animals are not made in God's image; therefore, they are not moral creatures and as such cannot marry. Since marriage is a moral decision based on law, love, respect, and commitment, it can apply only to moral beings. However, it is also important to know, that when man is raised from the dead, he is not raised in an earthly body, but a spiritual one; therefore, he will not marry but will be like the angels in heaven (1 Cor. 15:44; Matt. 22:30).

Mankind was made to rule over the creation of God. Dominion, or the act of ruling, was given to man, not to animals. In the eighth Psalm, verse six reads, "You have made him to have dominion over the works of Your hands; You have put all things under his feet." This truth is also seen in Genesis 2:15, where God placed the man in the Garden of Eden to "tend" (labor and serve) and "keep" (have charge or rule over). Animals are often captured, tamed, and trained to serve in some capacity under man. This is never reversed, where animals catch and tame men. Why? Because we are made in God's image, of course. We have the ability to plan and design, debate, communicate, recall information, appreciate beauty and order, while building and destroying things for advancement. Animals do not.

Mankind was made male and female for superior reasons than animals were made. Animals reproduce simply to keep their species alive (Gen. 7:3). While God made mankind with the ability to reproduce, it serves a higher purpose. Man was to fill the earth in order to subdue it (Gen. 1:28).

This relates to the importance of marriage. In order to reproduce in a way that was acceptable, God gave man a moral law which required a man to leave his father and mother and to be joined to his wife (Gen. 2:25). The family unit is God's choice for man to reproduce and develop spiritual training (Ps. 127; 128; Mal. 2:15; Is. 38:19).

FILL IN THE BLANK:

1. James 3:7, "For every _____ of beast and bird, of reptile and creature of the sea, is _____ and has been _____ by _____."

2. 1 Corinthians 15:49, "And as we have borne the image of the man of _____, we shall also bear the image of the _____ Man."

3. 2 Corinthians 5:10, "For we must _____ appear before the _____ seat of Christ, that each one may receive the things done in the _____, according to what he has done, whether _____ or _____."

4. Matthew 22:30, "For in the _____

"Then God blessed them, and God said to them, "Be fruitful and multiply; fill the earth and subdue it; have dominion over the fish of the sea, over the birds of the air, and over every living thing that moves on the earth."

(Gen. 1:28)

they neither _____ nor are given in _____, but are like _____ of God in heaven."

QUESTION:

5. Why is each man going to be judged for what he does in the body but animals are not? ____

_____

_____

> "Therefore a man shall leave his father and mother and be joined to his wife, and they shall become one flesh."
>
> (Gen. 2:24)

Man Marries and is Given in Marriage

From the Scriptures, we learn that marriage is an honorable and recognized union between one man and one woman who vow to live faithfully to each other before God until death separates them. Jesus endorsed this. He called His opponents back to the Genesis 2:24 law in Mark 10:6–9. He also attended a wedding in John 2. Animals cannot celebrate a marriage any more than they can enter one. Have you ever seen animals celebrate weddings? They do not have the capacity to act except by natural impulse and instinct. Man, however, is to be governed and restrain his passion with reason (2 Pet. 2:12).

The Want of Woman

Woman, like man, was made in the image of God; she alone is suitable for man (Gen. 1:27; 2:18–24). Genesis 1:31 brings the sixth day to an end with the complete satisfaction of God calling it "very good." This phrase is unique to the sixth day. The other days were "good," or *pleasant*, but it was only after what was created on day six that it was called "very" (exceedingly) good. This exceedingly good state did not exist until after woman was made.

Genesis 2 provides more detail of what went on during the sixth day. God had made Adam from

LESSON 3 In the Beginning — The Family

the dust of the ground, but the Lord expressed, "It is not good that man should be alone; I will make him a helper comparable to him" (Gen. 2:18). While man was made "good," the creation was still lacking until God, in His wisdom, fashioned that "helper" from Adam's side. What can we learn from this as it relates to the meaning and makeup of marriage?

> *Man and woman are historically connected.* Man and woman become "one flesh" sexually because they are one flesh historically (Gen. 2:21–24). This fundamentally destroys the homosexual idea. Homosexuality is rebellion against God's choice and denies the very reason why God made "male and female." Homosexuality is dishonorable, unnatural, vile, and shameful (Rom. 1:24–27).
>
> *Woman needs man.* Woman's beginning is from man (Gen. 2:22). Her origin begins from his side. This suggests her role in creation to be a submissive helper (1 Tim. 2:11–13).

- How does a woman help her husband? _____

- How does a woman show submission? _____

> *Man is dependent upon woman.* As long as there was no woman, man stood incomplete. She was created for him, and his continual survival is through her (1 Cor. 11:9, 11, 12). Man must understand and honor his wife (1 Pet. 3:7).

- How does one learn to understand his wife? _____

- How does a man honor his wife? _____

> *Woman is the helper for man.* God did not make another man to be a suitable helper; He made woman. This role should not be frowned on by either man or woman but viewed with honor. This word "helper" is most often used in Scripture of God as our *helper* (Ps. 33:20; 121:2, etc.).
>
> *Marriage is between one woman and one man.* God made only "two." Jesus said, "The two shall become one flesh" (Mk. 10:8; Matt. 19:5). Any

marriage that has more than one man and one woman violates God's model.

- Do you know any religions that allow more than one mate in a marriage? _____

  _____

- Does Jesus approve of such? _____

  _____

Marriage is the training ground for raising children. The last book of the Old Testament answers that God made man and woman to become one flesh because God wants parents to raise godly offspring (Mal. 2:15). Paul commanded fathers, "...but bring them up in the training and admonition of the Lord" (Eph. 6:4).

Marriage is a training ground for parents. Marriage calls us to grow beyond ourselves. The woman is called to respect her husband (Eph. 5:33). Marriage becomes a good place for her to continue to develop a meek and quiet spirit (1 Pet. 3:1-6). Man is called to understand and honor his wife (1 Pet. 3:7). He learns to think beyond himself and toward the needs of another. Parents also learn the sacrifice of having and raising children. It is no wonder that God wants the overseers of His church to be married men who have raised godly children (Titus 1:5-7).

- Does God want those who oversee His church to first learn to oversee their family? _____

  _____

- Can you name some things that your parents have sacrificed for you? _____

  _____

God has given one reason for a spouse to put away and remarry another— sexual immorality. Jesus instructed that fornication (sexual immorality) was a violation against marriage and served as the only ground for the innocent to put away one and remarry (Matt. 19:9). God created one man to be with one woman for life. Fornicators and adulterers will be judged (Heb. 13:4).

LESSON 3 In the Beginning — The Family

QUESTIONS:

6. Why is mankind able to marry while animals are not? _____
   _____
   _____
   _____

7. While God's creation was "good," what was not good about man in Genesis 2:18? _____
   _____
   _____
   _____

8. Name two reasons why woman is not to teach or have authority over man (1 Timothy 2:11–14). _____
   _____
   _____
   _____

9. Isaiah 38:19, "The living, the living man, he shall praise You, As I do this day; The _____ shall make known Your _____ to the _____."

10. A widow is a woman whose husband had died. How is remarriage seen as a spiritual help to young widows (1 Tim. 5:13, 14)? _____
    _____
    _____
    _____
    _____
    _____

Lesson 4

In the Beginning — Satan's Allurement

Genesis 3:1-6

Genesis chapter 3 shows us something terribly wrong with Adam and Eve from what we have seen in chapter 2. The couple is taken from an age of innocence and tending God's beautiful garden to being driven with shame, with fear, and eventually out of the Garden, away from the tree of life. Genesis shows us that sin is the reason for this change. But if sin is so bad, why would anyone commit a sin? Genesis shows us that there is more to the problem of sin than what meets the eye. It begins with the crafty serpent, and through the temptation of lies one is led away by personal desire. Sin has to become appealing for anyone to commit it, but its end is shame, pain, fear, suffering, sorrow, and death. It comes across as something exciting and pleasurable, but it is important to understand that sin always make you pay more than what you thought you would have to pay. Sin's price tag is death (Rom. 6:23). Sin is so costly, in fact, that it required a torturous death of God's own Son to provide a payment for our sins (Gal. 3:3, 4). In this lesson, we want to learn about the adversary of our souls, who allures us to sin.

FILL IN THE BLANK:

1. Romans 6:23, "For the _____ of _____ is _____, but the gift of God is eternal life in Christ Jesus our Lord."

Key Passage

"Now the serpent was more cunning than any beast of the field which the LORD God had made. And he said to the woman, 'Has God indeed said, "You shall not eat of every tree of the garden"?'"

(Gen. 3:1)

Satan—The Cunning Serpent (Gen. 3:1).

GENESIS 3:1

"Now the serpent was more cunning than any beast of the field which the LORD God had made. And he said to the woman, 'Has God indeed said, "You shall not eat of every tree of the garden"?'"

FILL IN THE BLANK:

2. Revelation 12:9, "So the great _____ was cast out, that _____ of old, called the _____ and _____, who deceives the whole world; he was cast to the earth, and his angels were cast out with him."

A literal serpent appeared to Eve, controlled by Satan. The apostle John identified the serpent as Satan. Jesus identified the devil as a liar and murderer from the beginning (Jn. 8:44). The serpent was a perfect choice in Satan's underhanded scheme due *to being cunning*. To be cunning is being crafty in a bad way. Rebekah had Jacob dress in Esau's clothes and put goat skin on his hands and neck, so he would appear to Jacob as Esau, hairy. Isaac's eyes had grown dim, and he was deceived, blessing Jacob as Esau. Without *craftiness*, the serpent could not deceive anyone. In the New Testament, some opponents of Christ were also cunning and tried to pretend they were righteous but were only seeking to trap Jesus (see Luke 20:20–26). We cannot overstate the crafty nature of Satan. He gives great thought into his

---

"Grace to you and peace from God the Father and our Lord Jesus Christ, who gave Himself for our sins, that He might deliver us from this present evil age, according to the will of our God and Father."

(Gal. 3:3, 4)

"But I fear, lest somehow, as the serpent deceived Eve by his craftiness, so your minds may be corrupted from the simplicity that is in Christ."

(2 Cor. 11:3)

choices to deceive and destroy. This cleverness is seen in his choice of a serpent and in his work to bring Adam down by first attacking Eve.

Satan Questions God's Word (Gen. 3:1).

Notice what Satan says to the woman in Genesis 3:1, "Has God indeed said, 'You shall not eat of every tree of the garden'?" Satan takes the commandments of God and frames them into *questions*. Why? Satan desires us to question God's word so that we will not heed and obey the warning.

QUESTIONS:

3. What might be some areas today where Satan wants us to turn God's commandments into questions?

    . What would Satan want you to do with the warning from God about evil friendships (1 Cor. 15:33)? _____
    _____
    _____

    . What would Satan want women to do with the command to not teach or have authority over a man (1 Tim. 2:12)?_____
    _____
    _____

    . What would Satan want men to do with the command to not lust after women (Prov. 6:25; Matt. 5:28)? _____
    _____
    _____

    . What would Satan want people to do with the statement that wine will mock us and lead us to acts of violence (Prov. 20:1)?_____
    _____
    _____

- What would Satan want those who have not obeyed the gospel to do with the teaching that we must act today and not trust in tomorrow (Prov. 27:1; 2 Cor. 6:2)? _____
  _____
  _____

4. From the following verses, what are some ways that we can safeguard our souls from being deceived by Satan's lies?

   - If we speak, what should we speak from what? 1 Peter 4:11. _____
     _____

   - On what should our thinking be centered? 1 Corinthians 4:6. _____
     _____
     _____

   - Read the second temptation of Jesus in Matthew 4:5–7. Did Satan use Scripture? _____ Did Satan use Scripture correctly? _____ Does God want us to throw ourselves down from high places to see if He will save us? _____ How did Jesus defeat Satan in this temptation? _____
     _____

     Must all Scripture agree with all Scripture? _____
     _____

Satan Contradicts God Word (Gen. 3:2–4).

Where God says, "You will surely die," Satan adds one word, *not*, which completely reverses what the Lord said. Satan wanted Eve to believe the opposite of what the Lord said. Where God has not placed a *not*, we should not add one. Where God has placed one, we should not take it away.

God has placed the requirement upon the overseers of the church to be married men with faithful children (Titus 1:6). Satan wants to put some *not's* in that passage and have us believe elders do not have to be men, they do not have to be married, and they do not have to have faithful children. God has commanded that we should not forsake the assembling of ourselves together (Heb. 10:25). Satan wants to strike out that *not* and have people justify themselves for choosing to forsake the services of the church. The Bible tells us to behold the goodness and the severity of God (Rom. 11:22). Satan wants to write in that God is not good, or on the other hand, that God is not severe. The Holy Spirit has said through the apostle Peter that "The like figure whereunto even baptism doth also now save us…" (1 Pet. 3:21, KJV). However, that unholy spirit, Satan, wants to change the word "now" to "not." He has hordes of preachers teaching everywhere that "baptism does not save us," but that "we are saved by faith alone." We need to beware of the *"not's"* in the devil's "tale" of lies.

Satan redefines the character of God (Gen. 3:5)

Satan challenges Eve's understanding of God. He tempts her by acting as a theologian on the character of God. He reveals something new to Eve, claiming that God was actually keeping something wonderful from her. He paints God as keeping Eve in the shadow of ignorance and indicates that she is simply unaware of all the power that is available for her in experiencing a life being "like God" if she eats.

Satan is the great deceiver and often pretends to be something which he is not (2 Cor. 11:13, 14). He would pretend that he is a messenger of light, but he is a liar, a deceiver, and a murderer. He wants us to believe that life is better if we disobey God. He wants us to believe that God is holding us down from experiencing the good life.

When someone says, "I am too young and have too many fun things to experience in life before I follow Jesus," that person believes Satan's lie that

> "For such are false apostles, deceitful workers, transforming themselves into apostles of Christ. And no wonder! For Satan himself transforms himself into an angel of light."
>
> (2 Cor. 11:13, 14)

life is more fun in disobeying God, as well as the lie that there will always be a tomorrow to obey God.

God's character is proven true through His sending of His own Son to die as a sacrifice for us. Life was taken away when Adam and Eve sinned, but Jesus taught, "The thief does not come except to steal, and to kill, and to destroy. I have come that they may have life, and that they may have it more abundantly" (Jn. 10:10). We can have life abundantly today by obedience; eventually eternal life is found when Jesus comes again (Col. 3:1–4).

Satan's Enticements (Gen. 3:6)

Why did Eve fall? She fell not only by "believing" the devil's lie but also by "desiring" what was spoken in the lie. "But each one is tempted when he is drawn away by his own desires and enticed" (Jas. 1:14). When one is drawn away by his "own" desires, one has left the desire to please God. The enticement to sin comes in three areas.

> "For all that is in the world—the lust of the flesh, the lust of the eyes, and the pride of life—is not of the Father but is of the world."
>
> (1 John 2:16)

QUESTIONS:

5. What are some of your temptations? _____
   _____
   _____
   _____

6. Are you tempted to disobey your parents? ___
   _____
   _____

7. Are you ever tempted to cheat, watch an inappropriate movie, speak bad language, wear immodest clothing? _____
   _____
   _____

8. What does God want you to do in those temptations? _____

_____

_____

_____

FILL IN THE BLANK:

9. James 4:7, "Therefore _____ to God. _____ the devil and he will flee from you."

Three Areas of Enticement

Lust of the Flesh

Eve saw that the *tree was good for food* and therefore desired to take it. This sin is repeated many times in the Bible. Esau gave away his birthright because of his desire for food (Gen. 25:29–34). On another occasion, Israel yielded to intense craving and tested God (Ps. 78:18; cf. Num. 11:4–35). Paul identified that those who walk according to Satan will seek to fulfill the lust of the flesh but are children of wrath (Eph. 2:1–3). The remedy is to put on Christ and make no provision for the flesh, to fulfill its wicked lust.

Lust of the Eyes

Eve fixed her eyes on the *pleasant* appearance of the fruit and therefore desired to take it. This sin works through covetousness. Achan saw and coveted a beautiful garment along with some silver and gold, and took them (Josh. 7:21). David beheld his neighbor's wife, Bathsheba, and then took her (2 Sam. 11:2–4). It all started with a "look." Jesus warned men to not look in lust (Matt. 5:28). As a remedy, we should quickly bounce our eyes off of something which would make us lust and focus our attention on something else. We ought to look at what is *unseen* to our naked eyes (such as God, heaven, hell, angels, the coming judgment, Jesus' death on the cross, etc.) and move with fear and trembling (see 2 Cor. 4:18; Heb. 11:25–27).

Pride of Life

Eve was motivated by pride in becoming wise. The wise man warned, "Pride goes before destruction, And a haughty spirit before a fall" (Prov. 16:18). As a remedy to pride, humility (lowliness of mind) is needed. We never outgrow the need to continue growing in grace and knowledge. Humility is

36 In the Beginning — The Creation

seen in this admonition, "And if anyone thinks that he knows anything, he knows nothing yet as he ought to know" (1 Cor. 8:2).

WORD APPLICATION: *humility*

10. Define humility in your own words (Phil. 2:3 and Rom. 12:3, 16)? _____

_____

_____

_____

11. What is the opposite of humility? _____

_____

_____

_____

12. In Titus 3:2, Paul commanded Christians to show humility to all men.

    . How would you view yourself with pride versus humility? _____

    _____

    _____

    . How might you view others if you are filled with pride versus humility?__

    _____

    . How would you show humility when someone insults you? _____

    _____

    _____

    . How would you show humility when your parents are trying to teach you something?_____

    _____

    _____

LESSON 4 In the Beginning — Satan's Allurement

- How would you show humility to your teacher and other students in Bible class? _____
_____
_____

- How would you show humility during a sermon when the gospel is being preached? _____
_____
_____

- How would you show humility to those who disagree with you? _____
_____
_____

FILL IN THE BLANK:

13. Proverbs 30:6, "Do not _____ to His _____, Lest He rebuke you, and you be found a _____."

QUESTIONS:

14. What word does Satan add to God's word in Genesis 3:4? _____
_____

15. Name the three areas of temptation. _____
_____
_____

16. What are some things Paul advised for us to do as a help against pride in Romans 12:16? _____
_____
_____

17. Moses taught Israel that God was their life. What three things did Moses counsel the children of Israel to do toward God to have life in Deuteronomy 30:20? Should we do those things today? _____

    _____

    _____

18. Read 2 Corinthians 4:18 and finish out this verse, "While we do not look at the things which are seen..." _____

    _____

    _____

    _____

TRUE OR FALSE:

    T or F   Eve was forced to disobey God's word.

    T or F   Adam was forced to take the fruit from Eve and eat it.

    T or F   Satan appears as an angel of light.

    T or F   If something looks good, we should go ahead and take it for ourselves.

In the Beginning — Sin and Its Consequences

Genesis 3:7-24

Genesis 3:7–24 underscores man's underlying problem—*sin!* Many of the problems we face in life are only temporary and are limited to life on earth. Diseases and physical weaknesses affect the body now, but these have no effect on the life to come.

Sin, however, is something that destroys the soul into eternity. In Romans 6:23, Paul reveals, "For the wages of sin is death…" While Genesis shows that the presence of sin in this world has brought real physical curses, it underscores that the most important consequence of sin is being separated from God. This results in eternal death.

What is sin? The Bible defines sin as lawlessness. The apostle John wrote, "Whoever commits sin also commits lawlessness, and sin is lawlessness" (1 Jn. 3:4). In fact, "All unrighteousness is sin…" (1 Jn. 5:17). Sin is not necessarily something visible but is played out in actions that break God's law. It is similar to when your parent tells you to do your Bible lesson, clean your room, and do your homework. If you only do two of the three things but act as if you have done all three, then you have lied. The lie is the action of lawlessness. Likewise, our society often ignores, justifies, and redefines sin. When sin is committed in acts of lying, cheating, adultery, murder, homosexuality, alcoholism, etc., it is often redefined as "abnormal," "alternative," "insane," "an affair," or just a "sickness." Regardless of what people call it, God calls it "sin," which is "lawlessness" and

Key Passage

"For the wages of sin is death, but the gift of God is eternal life in Christ Jesus our Lord."

(Rom. 6:23)

"unrighteousness." Since every sin breaks God's law, those who practice sin make themselves *enemies* of God (Rom. 5:10).

On the other hand, righteousness is known through God's word. We make ourselves *friends* of God when we obey His commandments. "My tongue shall speak of Your word, For all Your commandments are righteousness" (Ps. 119:172).

QUESTIONS

1. What does sin break? Give scripture. _____
   _____

2. What is the ultimate consequence of sin? Give scripture. _____
   _____

3. Who is accepted by God (Acts 10:34, 35)?_____
   _____

4. Where is the righteousness of God found today (Rom. 1:16, 17)?_____

5. See 1 Corinthians 6:9–11.

    a. Will the unrighteous inherit the kingdom of God? _____
       _____

    b. Name some forms of unrighteousness. _____
       _____
       _____

    c. Can people who are living in unrighteousness change and start living for Christ? _____
       _____
       _____
       _____

LESSON 5 In the Beginning — Sin and Its Consequences

Five Things About Sin (Gen. 3:7–24)

Sin Brings Shame (Gen. 3:7).

After heeding Satan's words, Adam and Eve quickly learned that it was not good "knowing good and evil." Their lives in the Garden of Eden were no longer enjoyable but became plagued with fear and shame. They scurried to find themselves anything with which to cover their nakedness. *Shame* and *nakedness* are often found together in Scripture. Isaiah penned in 47:3, "Your nakedness shall be uncovered, Yes, your shame will be seen; I will take vengeance, And I will not arbitrate with a man." When nakedness is uncovered, shame is seen. Jesus told the church in Laodicea, "I counsel you to buy from Me...white garments, that you may be clothed, that the shame of your nakedness may not be revealed..." (Rev. 3:18). We should be ashamed to have others look at us when we are not wearing enough clothes (physical nakedness). When we have sin ruling in our lives, we appear as if we are naked before God (spiritual nakedness). How much more should we feel shame when all our crimes against God's law are being seen by God? This is why all men need to have their sins forgiven by God so they can stand before Him as if they are clothed in righteousness. In baptism, our sins are washed away, and we are clothed with Christ (Acts 22:16; Gal. 3:27). However, sin can have a hardening effect to dull the sense of shame. Much of what is praised as fashionable (short skirts, short shorts, bikinis, low cut shirts, etc.) is viewed as lawlessness to God.

6. In _____ the prophet warned his people of a coming punishment which was caused by their inability to blush (be ashamed).

> "Behold, the LORD'S hand is not shortened, That it cannot save; Nor His ear heavy, That it cannot hear. But your iniquities have separated you from your God; And your sins have hidden His face from you, So that He will not hear."
>
> (Is. 59:1, 2)

Sin Brings Separation from God (Gen. 3:8-10, 22-24)

The most destructive effect of sin is that it places a divide between God and us. This separation is seen graphically when the first couple hid from the presence of the Lord (Gen. 3:8-10). Since they still felt shame and fear, they discovered the coverings they made from fig leaves were inadequate. Even though they were wearing something, they still felt naked. Man cannot fix the problem of sin by himself. He must have God's help.

Sin not only makes us want to hide from God, but it also makes God want to hide His face from us (Is. 59:1, 2; 64:7). The word *separate* carries with it the idea of a divide. Jeremiah pictured this separation as God covering Himself with a cloud so that prayer would not pass through to Him (Lam. 3:44). God hides His face and cannot pardon those who indulge in sin.

Jesus taught in a parable of a father who had a very rebellious son who demanded his inheritance (Lk. 15:11-24). His father gave it to him, but he would not encourage his son's ways. His son knew this and journeyed to what Jesus called "a far country" and wasted his possessions with *prodigal*, or *wild* and *unruly*, living (Lk. 15:13). When we choose to indulge in sin, we actually journey far away from God. But if we can discover guilt for our crimes and repent, we can be restored to the Father even as this young man was.

Sin Brings the Tendency to Justify Wrongdoing (Gen. 3:11-13)

When Adam was asked if he had eaten from the tree, he shifted the blame away from himself to the woman. Satan would like us to deceive ourselves from our error by shifting the focus onto someone else thereby excusing self. While Adam was not deceived, he still disobeyed God by participating in Eve's sin. Turning the focus on the "woman God gave him" did not help him. Blaming Eve for giving him the fruit was no excuse. She could not force him to eat. Likewise, God had no part in his fall by giving Adam a woman. God does not tempt anyone with evil (Jas. 1:13-15). It was wholly Adam's choice to sin. It is an often-repeated crime today for people in sin to shift the blame to someone else.

Eve followed the course of her husband and shifted the focus on the serpent, but she had more humility in confessing that she was deceived. Yet, let us appreciate that "confessing we were deceived" will not bring about forgiveness and reconciliation with God. Sin is always against God. Confessing the faults of others or exaggerating the details of the circumstances or trying to cover up our sin with good intentions have all been tried by people in the Bible and all have failed (see Aaron, Exod. 32:22-24; Saul, 1 Sam. 13:12, 13; Pharaoh Exod. 9:27-35).

We must confess our *sins*, not *circumstances* that we sinned in (1 Jn. 1:9, 10). Confessing, "I grew up in a hard environment," "the devil made me do it," "I was made this way," "the circumstances in my life are too hard to do right," etc. is barren of mercy and charges God with being a liar. His word tells us that God will not allow us to be tempted beyond what we are able.

FILL IN THE BLANK:

7. 1 Corinthians 10:13, "No _____ has overtaken you except such as is _____ to man; but God is faithful, who will not _____ you to be tempted beyond what you are able, but with the temptation will also make the way of _____, that you may be able to _____ it."

If we find ourselves being a prisoner of war with Satan, it is because we willfully gave in to him. Let us own up to our sin like the young prodigal: "...Father, I have sinned against heaven and before you, and I am no longer worthy to be called your son. Make me like one of your hired servants" (Lk. 15:18, 19). This conveys both the recognition of the sin and the genuine determination to repent. This is set in contrast to the person who gets angry at rebuke and detaches himself from the congregation. "A man who isolates himself seeks his own desire; He rages against all wise judgment" (Pr. 18:1).

Sin Brings Curses (Gen. 3:14–19)

The key word in this section is *curse* (Gen. 3:14, 17). Sin brings a curse. A curse is an evil, a misfortune, or a punishment. The excuses offered up had no impact on God's judgment. The serpent was cursed to move on his belly and eat dust all the

> "He who covers his sins will not prosper, But whoever confesses and forsakes them will have mercy."
>
> (Prov. 28:13)

days of his life. The serpent tempted Eve to eat, so it seemed fitting for him to travel on his *belly*. It is implied in Genesis 3:14 that all creatures are cursed, but the serpent more so. This curse may also amplify Adam and Eve's transgression. The serpent, which presented himself as wise, would no longer appear that way, slithering on his belly in the dirt.

There was also enmity (a hostile conflict) that the serpent would have with the woman and specifically between his seed and her seed. Eve was already at enmity with the serpent by his deceiving her. This battle would eventually be between Satan and the Christ, who was born of a woman without a human father (Gal. 4:4; 1 Jn. 3:8). It is also waged down through time by those who rebel against God's commandments versus those who take up the good fight and expose error. These righteous ones defeat deceptive flattery even as the church in Rome did, by marking and avoiding those who cause divisions (Rom. 16:17–20).

Despite being deceived, Eve would also be cursed with physical consequences (Gen. 3:16). Her punishment was directed to her being a mother and wife. God would greatly vex her in mind and body by multiplying her sorrow in conception and pain in childbearing.

Adam was also going to suffer (Gen. 3:17–19). Rather than tending the luscious Garden, he would till the ground, and by hard toil, it would produce thorns and thistles to hamper his harvest. Death was also pronounced, as he would return to the dust from which he was taken after the couple was driven away from the tree of life (Gen. 3:22–24).

Sin Requires a Covering (Gen. 3:21)

While Adam and Eve would continue to bear the physical consequences of their sin, God would remove the shame by providing a covering for their nakedness. God provided tunics for them. These tunics were modest and would have covered the shoulders down to the knees. Likewise, we should give great consideration to our clothing (1 Tim. 2:9, 10). Ask, "Does my clothing display godliness or nakedness?"

These tunics were made from a blood sacrifice as is implied by "skin." God did not create these out of nothing, but *made* them from animal hide. There is both physical and spiritual nakedness that we must cover. The *tunic* covered the physical nakedness; the *skin* foreshadowed the need to cover the spiritual nakedness by blood. Introduced here is a prevailing theme of the Bible: *Something must die to cover my sin* (Heb. 9:22). The Lamb of God would eventually come to take away our sins by His own blood sacrifice and provide a covering for the soul (Jn. 1:29; Rev. 1:5; Gal. 3:27).

LESSON 5 In the Beginning — Sin and Its Consequences

QUESTIONS:

8. Did Adam and Eve's feelings of shame go away after they made themselves coverings? Why or why not_____
_____
_____

9. Can one be wearing something and still be considered naked (Gen. 3:7, 10)? Why or why not? _____
_____

10. What do you think is the worst of all sin's consequences? _____
_____

11. Does offering excuses for our sins justify us before God? What are some excuses you have offered to your parents when you disobeyed? Did those excuses justify you before your parents?_____
_____

12. What did Eve confess was the reason for her sin?_____
_____

13. What are some excuses that men give to justify their sins?_____
_____
_____
_____

14. In Psalm 41:4, what did David pray would be healed, since he had sinned?_____
_____
_____
_____

15. What is a curse? What punishment or misfortune have you suffered from a sin you have committed? _____
_____
_____
_____
_____

16. The kind of clothing we wear communicates something about us. What does the clothing in Proverbs 7:10 and 2 Samuel 13:18, 19 tell about the people? Describe the kind of clothing that should be worn to play sports, to school, to worship. What kind of clothing should not be worn?
_____
_____
_____
_____
_____
_____
_____
_____

17. How are we clothed spiritually from sin today? See Galatians 3:26, 27. ___
_____
_____
_____
_____

In the Beginning — Sin and Its Corruption of Worship, Brotherly Love, and the Family — Genesis 4

In Genesis Chapter 4, we continue to see the far-reaching effects of sin on man while living outside the Garden of Eden. In this chapter we are introduced to the first three male children of Adam and Eve.

The First Two Brothers (Gen. 4:1, 2)

Eve considered her ability to bear children as a blessing from God. She did not harbor grudges against the Lord for sending her out of paradise but praised Him for her ability to bring forth a child. Likewise, all women would do well to remember that it is God who gives life in the womb. Aborting that life is killing a life from God.

FILL IN THE BLANK:

1. Psalms 127:3, "Behold, _____ are a heritage from the LORD, The _____ of the _____ is a _____."

The occupation of the first two sons consisted of Cain being a tiller of the ground and Abel being a shepherd. Tilling the ground would have been very hard labor. The ground had already been cursed and would not yield the full strength of produce it had originally been designed to do (Gen. 3:17, 18). Cain was a hard worker, which is a positive quality (2 Tim. 2:6). Man was created to work, and being lazy is a sin.

Key Passage

"God is Spirit, and those who worship Him must worship in spirit and truth."

(John 4:24)

FILL IN THE BLANK:

2. 2 Thessalonians 3:10, "For even when we were with you, we _____ you this: If anyone will not _____, neither shall he _____."

As a shepherd, Abel could have provided clothing for Adam's race. His occupation, as we will see, also provided the acceptable sacrifices unto the Lord.

The Corruption of Worship (Gen 4:3–5)

Genesis 4:3–5 and the importance of true worship.

We learn several lessons from these few verses and should be impressed with how important worship is. Jesus told the woman at the well that the Father seeks "true worshipers" (Jn. 4:23). Genesis 4 should drive the point home that God never seeks or approves of false worship.

- The very first conflict between brothers is over worship.
- Worship is either *respectable* or *unrespectable*. Not all worship is acceptable. To have respectable worship requires one to know God's will and be willing to reproduce that will in your life. Paul told the Christians in Rome to "...present your bodies a living sacrifice, holy, acceptable to God, which is your reasonable service" (Rom. 12:1, emp. added).
- God respects men by the kind of worship they give. Notice that the Lord "respected Abel and his offering." He *did not respect* Cain or his offering.

FILL IN THE BLANK:

3. Genesis 4:4, 5, "Abel also brought of the firstborn of his flock and of their fat. And the LORD _____ Abel and his _____, but He did not _____ Cain and his _____. And Cain was very angry, and his countenance fell."

True worship is not necessarily measured by the amount of work that is put into it. Cain could have argued that he had worked harder for his offering than did his brother Abel.

True worship is offered up by faith. The New Testament tells us that *by faith*, Abel offered to God a more excellent sacrifice (Heb. 11:4). Does this mean that Abel simply believed in his sacrifice more than Cain did his? No. We are told that faith comes by hearing the word of God in Romans 10:17. Therefore to do something *by faith* is to do something by the directions of the word of God. This means Abel had been instructed by the Lord and he obeyed. Because of this, he received the witness or testimony from God that he was righteous. *Righteousness* is connected to keeping God's commandments (see Deut. 6:25; Ps. 119:172; Lk. 1:6; 2 Pet. 2:21). God approved of Abel and his worship because he obeyed God's commandments.

The worship God wants today.

Worship matters today. We should develop the humility to ask, "Is my worship better than Cain's?" What kind of worship does God want today?

> Preaching. God desires that we listen to what the apostles have written for us (1 Cor. 4:6).

FILL IN THE BLANK:

4. Acts 2:42, "And they continued steadfastly in the apostles' _____ and fellowship, in the breaking of bread, and in prayers."

We will be judged by the word of Christ, so it makes sense for us to know it (Jn. 12:48). Preaching and teaching help us know the will of God and such is an act of worship rendered unto God.

> Fellowship. *Fellowship* means to share in something. Paul penned in 2 Corinthians 6:14, "Do not be unequally yoked together with unbelievers. For what fellowship has righteousness with lawlessness? And what

"So then faith comes by hearing, and hearing by the word of God."

(Rom. 10:17)

communion has light with darkness?" Can you see how righteousness has no *share* or *fellowship* with lawlessness, even as light has nothing to *share* with darkness? *Fellowship* is translated "share" in the New King James version or "communicate" in the King James Version, in Hebrew 13:16. Fellowship with God is based on what is right. Christians are called into the fellowship of God's Son (1 Cor. 1:9). We cannot maintain fellowship with God and other saints if we walk in darkness (Eph. 5:11; 1 Jn. 1:3–7). Paul taught that fellowship requires God's children to be *like-minded* (Phil. 2:1, 2). This is a mindset that strives together for the faith of the gospel and learns to think like Jesus thought (Phil. 1:27, 2:5). Three kinds of attitudes are needed to have fellowship with God.

> *A humble and obedient attitude (Phil. 2:3, 7, 8).* It is only by humble obedience that we can be pleasing to God.
>
> *A persistent clinging to the word of life (Phil. 2:14–16).* Our energies must always respond from what we read in the word. If we separate from the word, we walk away from life. Without the word of life, we cannot have the same mind toward one another or know the mind of Christ.
>
> *A willingness to suffer (Phil. 1:29).* These brethren were to know that suffering was a part of having the mind of Christ (Phil. 2:8). They knew that Paul and Epaphroditus suffered (Phil. 2:17, 1:16; 2:25–30). So we must seek to know and share in Christ's suffering (Phil. 3:10).

Lord's Supper. God desires that we remember the death of His Son each first day of the week (Acts 2:42; Acts 20:7).

FILL IN THE BLANK:

5. 1 Corinthians 11:26, "For as often as you _____ this bread and _____ this cup, you _____ the Lord's death till He comes."

It makes sense that if we are called into the fellowship of the death of His Son that we also continue to center our minds upon His death in a memorial.

> Prayer. God desires that we pray together (Acts 2:42). By prayer we share our burdens, concerns, hopes, and fears with the Lord. The early church had constant prayer (Acts 12:12).

LESSON 6 In the Beginning — Sin and Its Corruption of Worship, Brotherly Love, and the Family — Genesis

FILL IN THE BLANK:

6. Acts 12:5, "Peter was therefore kept in prison, but constant _____ was offered to God for him by the _____."

7. Singing. God _____ that we sing songs of _____ (Eph. 5:19; Heb. 13:15).

8. Colossians 3:16, "Let the word of Christ dwell in you richly in all wisdom, _____ and _____ one another in psalms and hymns and spiritual songs, _____ with grace in your hearts to the Lord."

These songs admonish one another as well as honor God. Despite the fact that God desires *a cappella*, or music without instruments, many want to add the music of their preference. But our worship must be what God wants lest we become guilty of wrong worship and sin like Cain. Worship has always been a test for man, and it reveals the current standing of a person's heart to God (Matt. 15:7–9).

QUESTIONS:

9. What two things did Jesus say we must do in order to have acceptable worship unto God in John 4:24? In your words, what do you think these two things mean? _____

10. Why was Abel's sacrifice acceptable while Cain's was not? _____

11. What three things did James command brethren in James 1:19, 20? _____

12. Name the five acts of worship with the Scriptures from the New Testament. _____
_____
_____

13. In your words, define *fellowship*. _____
_____
_____

14. Is our fellowship with God seen in our giving of our means on the first day of the week (1 Cor. 16:1, 2)? _____
_____

15. How did the church at Philippi have fellowship with Paul in Philippians 4:14–16? _____
_____

16. After instituting the Lord's Supper, what did Jesus and His disciples do? See Matthew 26:30. _____
_____

17. What kind of worship is it when we teach the commandments of men (Matt. 15:7–9)? _____
_____

The Danger of Anger (Gen. 4:6)

While anger by itself is not wrong, when it is misdirected or uncontrolled, it is sinful. Cain should have been angry with himself, but rather he was angry with God and Abel. We can learn three simple points from these two verses: 1) Cain's anger was not hidden from God, 2) Cain could have done what was right if he would have humbled himself, and 3) sin is always at the door, and it is easy to fall into it when we are angry.

The Corruption of Brotherly Love (Gen. 4:7–15)

The effects of sin are seen in how it affected the brotherly relationship of Cain and Abel. When you look at Cain, observe:

- He offered false worship (Gen. 4:3–5).
- He became angry at the truth (Gen. 4:6).
- He was unwilling to rule over the tendency to sin (Gen. 4:7).
- He murdered his brother Abel (Gen. 4:8).
- He murdered Abel because he hated him (1 Jn. 3:10–15).
- He lied about Abel's whereabouts, saying, "I do not know" (Gen. 4:9).
- He showed no remorse for his dead brother, by asking God, "Am I my brother's keeper?" *Note*: The Hebrew word for *keeper* means to guard, to watch over, and to protect.

Where sin exists, proper love does not. Cain had lost his love for God, which led to his departure from God's word and unconcern toward Abel. The love of God should become an influence to lead us away from being hateful and sway us to do what is good (see Titus 3:3, 4, 8).

The Corruption of the Family (Gen. 4:16–24)

Cain left the presence of the Lord to live as a vagabond or wanderer. Where did Cain get his wife? It should be understood that Cain's wife would have likely been one of his sisters, a daughter of Adam and Eve. No other people lived on earth and since Eve is the mother of all living, Cain had to take a descendant from Eve to be his wife (Gen. 3:20; 5:4). The same would have been true of Noah's grandchildren hundreds of years later, after the flood. This was not wrong for early man. It continued to be permissible until the Law of Moses came.

While Cain's descendants were skillful, they were also reckless. The Genesis 2:24 model of one man being bound to one woman was desecrated, (to treat a sacred place or thing with violent disrespect; violate), through Lamech, Cain's great, great, great grandson. He not only trampled on the law of marriage but continued the bloodshed and arrogance of Cain by killing a young man for merely wounding him. Sin surely has a terrible and destructive effect upon man's life.

We do not leave the chapter in complete darkness, however. We find another man who was born to Adam, Seth (Gen. 4:25, 26).

Eve's belief in God's promise in Genesis 3:15 is seen as continuing through Seth, who replaced Abel due to Cain killing him. *Seth* means "compensation." The significant accomplishment through Seth was not materialistic but spiritual: "Then men began to call on the name of the Lord." When our life is over on this earth, the only thing that will matter is if we also called on His name (Acts 22:16).

QUESTIONS:

18. Cain didn't believe he was his brother's keeper. Are we to be our brother's keeper? How might we as Christians be a keeper of other Christians? See 1 Thessalonians 5:14, 15 and Galatians 6:1–6 and state what we might need to do for our brethren in order to watch out for them? _____
_____
_____
_____

19. Cain thought he got away with murdering his brother. Does God always know our sins or can we hide them from Him? Explain why Cain thought he had gotten away with murder?_____
_____
_____
_____
_____
_____

20. Think of some lessons from the killing of Abel which apply to us today. How do we call upon the name of the Lord today?_____
_____
_____
_____

Lesson 7

In the Beginning — Sin and Its Epitaph

Genesis 5

In our studies, we see three primary consequences of sin. Sin separates man from God (Gen. 3). Sin separates brothers (Gen. 4). Sin brings physical death (Gen. 5). This lesson on Genesis Chapter 5 gives us the epitaph of sin—DEATH. Do you know what an epitaph is? An epitaph is a short inscription on a tombstone or monument that is important or related to the person who died. Some people have lived such terrible lives that their epitaph reads very negatively. A man named Jehoram would serve as an example of this. His biblical epitaph reads:

> "He was thirty-two years old when he became king. He reigned in Jerusalem eight years and, to no one's sorrow, departed" (2 Chron. 21:20).

No one loved him while he lived, and no one was sad to see him depart. Others lived and died with a completely different epitaph. This is what is said in 2 Chronicles 24:15, 16 about Jehoiada, a really good priest:

> "But Jehoiada grew old and was full of days, and he died; he was one hundred and thirty years old when he died. And they buried him in the City of David among the kings, because he had done good in Israel, both toward God and His house."

If sin were given an epitaph, it would be something like: "Sin entered the world, and death through sin" (Rom. 5:12). Or it might read something like, "The wages of sin is death" (Rom. 6:23).

Key Passage

"Therefore, just as through one man sin entered the world, and death through sin, and thus death spread to all men, because all sinned."

(Rom. 5:12)

Genesis Chapter 5 is a genealogy, or "family tree." Your parents, grandparents, and great-grandparents are a part of your genealogy. Genesis 5 contains the family history from Adam to Noah through Adam's son, Seth. If every person in the world today could trace his or her genealogy back through time, it would eventually have Noah's name recorded in it!

The genealogy in Genesis 5 has two purposes. First, it shows us that God keeps His word. God told Adam that if he were to eat of the tree of knowledge, he would die (Gen. 2:16, 17). Adam experienced spiritual death that very day. He also began to feel the effects of physical death as he began to grow old and eventually die. With the exception of Enoch, Genesis 5 stresses that each man lived so many years and then "he died." The second point is to show us how God is keeping His promise of preserving history through which the Seed (Jesus) would come, spoken of in Genesis 3:15. The Seed (Jesus) who would defeat the serpent would come through Seth. The New Testament traces Jesus' genealogy all the way back through Noah and even to Adam (Lk. 3:23–38).

QUESTIONS:

1. Name the fathers that make up Noah's family from Jared to Noah.

   Jared → _____ → _____ → _____ → Noah.

2. How old was Adam when he died? _____

3. What descendant of Seth is on record as living the longest on earth? ___

4. What descendant never died but was taken by God? _____

WALKING AWAY FROM GOD

There is a connection that exists between Genesis Chapters 4 and 5. We find two distinct family trees. Cain's genealogy is in Genesis 4. Seth's genealogy is in Genesis 5. While physical death affected both Cain's and Seth's descendants, Cain's family tree would eventually perish in the flood of Noah.

LESSON 7 In the Beginning — Sin and Its Epitaph

Let us consider Cain's family tree. He has a son named Enoch (Gen. 4:17). Cain builds a city and dedicates it to Enoch, which is noteworthy. His descendants excelled in worldly advancement in cattle, musical instruments, and tools; however, they continued growing corrupt and walking contrary to God. One person named Lamech decided to change God's design of marriage and decided to marry two women! He also murdered a young man and boasted of it in Genesis 4:23, 24. The spiritual state of Cain's family tree is miserable. You might ask, "Why did all of Cain's descendants perish in the judgment of water?" It was because they chose a path that walked away from God. Cain's decision to walk away from God not only affected him, but also his children and their children, and their children's children, etc. The prophet Amos spoke of the tragedy of how children had listened to the lies of their fathers and how it led them away from the commandments of God (Amos 2:4). Likewise, Jesus asked, "Can the blind lead the blind? Will they not both fall into the ditch?" (Lk. 6:9). If parents are blind to God's law, how can they raise their children in righteousness? What we are will have an influence on what others will become.

QUESTIONS:

5. Identify two names from Cain's family tree and Seth's family tree that had the same name (Gen. 4:17, 18; 5:21–25)? _____
_____

6. Where does walking away from God lead a person? _____
_____

7. How important is it for parents to teach their children the truth? Why? __
_____
_____
_____

8. "But did He not make them _____, Having a remnant of the Spirit? And why? _____ He seeks _____. Therefore take heed to your spirit, And let none deal treacherously with the wife of his youth" (Mal. 2:15, NKJV).

> "After he begot Methuselah, Enoch walked with God three hundred years, and had sons and daughters. So all the days of Enoch were three hundred and sixty-five years. And Enoch walked with God; and he was not, for God took him."
>
> (Gen. 5:22–24)

9. How thankful should you be if you have godly parents? _____

_____

10. Name some ways that ungodly parents hinder their children from knowing the Lord. _____

_____

_____

Walking with God

Unlike the physical accomplishments of Cain's descendants, Genesis 4:26 reads, "And as for Seth, to him also a son was born; and he named him Enoch. Then men began to call on the name of the LORD." The Bible speaks of no worldly accomplishments here, but rather of a call for faithful living by calling on the name of the Lord. This does not mean that every person in Seth's family tree was godly, but a deep reverence was found in the descendants, "Enoch" and "Noah." Of Noah, Genesis 6:9 reads, "... Noah was a just man, perfect in his generations. Noah walked with God." Likewise, of Enoch, it states that he "walked with God" (Gen. 5:24). What made Enoch remarkable was not having something built up and dedicated *to* him (as Cain did to Enoch in Genesis 4), but rather having something dedicated *in* him—*a deep faith that walked with God*. Note some contrasting qualities of the two. This chart shows some comparisons between these two men.

Let us note some things about the Enoch in Genesis 5 that make him remarkable.

- He was the father of Methuselah, the person on record as living longer than anyone else, at 969 years.

- The Seed promise; fulfilled in Jesus Christ is preserved through him (Lk. 3:23–38).

LESSON 7 In the Beginning — Sin and Its Epitaph 59

- Despite living in the same generation as Lamech in Genesis 4, Enoch was very concerned with God's word; he walked with God and condemned the ungodliness of his time. "Now Enoch, the seventh from Adam, prophesied about these men also, saying, 'Behold, the Lord comes with ten thousands of His saints, to execute judgment on all, to convict all who are ungodly among them of all their ungodly deeds which they have committed in an ungodly way, and of all the harsh things which ungodly sinners have spoken against Him'" (Jude 1:14, 15).

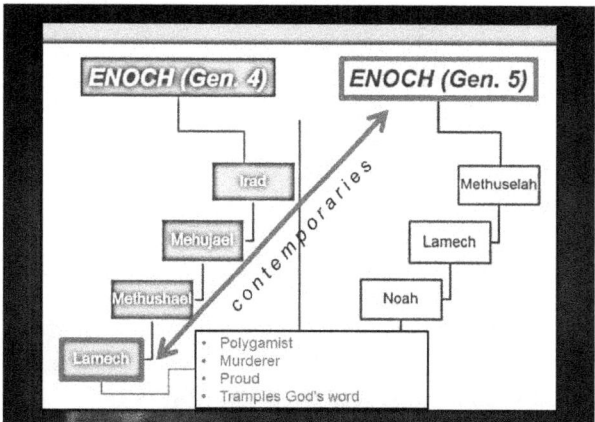

- Enoch is listed with the heroes of faith in Hebrews 11.

- Enoch did not die. Hebrews 11:5 reads, "By faith Enoch was taken away so that he did not see death, 'and was not found, because God had taken him'; for before he was taken he had this testimony, that he pleased God."

- Enoch pleased God, walking by faith. Genesis 5 tells us that Enoch walked with God, and Hebrews 11:5 tells us he had the testimony that he pleased God. When we please God, we are walking with God.

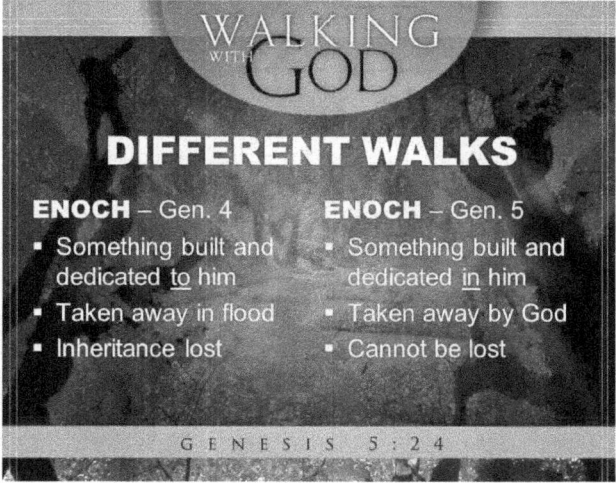

Walking with God requires that we agree with Him and His word. The prophet Amos penned in Amos 3:3, "Can two walk together, unless they are agreed?" We can be pleasing to God today by hearing and obeying His word even as Enoch did.

PRACTICAL APPLICATION:

11. When we hear and obey our parents, how do they react? _____
_____

12. Name something your parents told you to do and you obeyed. _____
_____
_____

13. How did you feel when you obeyed? _____
_____

14. How did you parents react to your obedience? _____
_____
_____

15. Did they "expect" you to obey? _____
_____

Jesus promised, "...If anyone loves Me, he will keep My word; and My Father will love him, and We will come to him and make Our home with him. He who does not love Me does not keep My words; and the word which you hear is not Mine but the Father's who sent Me" (Jn. 14:23, 24).

Enoch is also an example of being rewarded by God for walking with Him. The New Testament further notes, "But without faith it is impossible to please Him, for he who comes to God must believe that He is, and that He is a rewarder of those who diligently seek Him" (Heb. 11:6). God rewarded Enoch for his walk of faith.

He will also reward those who walk by faith throughout the ages by raising them from the dead when His Son comes again. Jesus told Martha after her brother died that "...I am the resurrection and the life. He who believes in Me, though he may die, he shall live" (Jn. 11:25). Won't it be a wonderful day when we are all raised from the grave and gain a victory over death, where we will never die again and never have sorrow, loneliness, pain, and disease? It will be wonderful for the living people who are faithful when Jesus comes again too! Like Enoch, they will be taken by God and will not suffer death and be able to ever live with Jesus! "Even so, come, Lord Jesus!" (Rev. 22:20).

QUESTIONS:

16. Fill in the blanks: 1 Thessalonians 4:17, "Then we who are _____ and _____ shall be _____ up together with them in the clouds to meet the Lord in the air. And thus we shall _____ be with the Lord."

17. What does it mean to walk by faith? Use Hebrews 11 to write what these faith heroes did to please God in their walk of faith.

    a. Abel (Heb. 11:4) _____
    _____

    b. Enoch (Heb. 11:5, 6) _____
    _____

    c. Noah (Heb. 11:7) _____
    _____

    d. Abraham (Heb. 11:8, 17–19) _____
    _____

18. From the following passages, what are some commandments we must do to be pleasing to God today?

    a. John 8:24 _____
    _____

62   In the Beginning — The Creation

    b. Acts 17:30 _____

    _____

    c. Matthew 10:32 _____

    _____

    d. Acts 2:38_____

    _____

    e. Revelation 2:10 _____

    _____

    f. Romans 13:1 _____

    _____

    g. Ephesians 6:1–3 _____

    _____

    h. Hebrews 13:16_____

    _____

    i. 1 John 1:6, 7 _____

    _____

19. From the following passages, what are some things we are commanded not to do?

    a. Hebrews 10:25 _____

    _____

    b. Ephesians 5:11_____

    _____

c. John 7:24 _____
_____

d. Romans 12:2 _____
_____

e. Romans 12:16 _____
_____

f. Romans 12:21 _____
_____

g. 1 Corinthians 15:33 _____
_____

h. Hebrews 3:8 _____
_____

i. 1 John 2:15 _____
_____

j. 3 John 1:11 _____
_____

Lesson 8

In the Beginning — Sin and Its Epitaph

Genesis 6

Genesis Chapter 6 shows sin's rapid advancement among mankind. Like a cancerous tumor which destroys the body, sin corrupts and perverts man. So have you noticed the major point of the Bible? How connected is sin to the Bible's overall message? The Bible records and preserves the history of sin. We should see it as the history book of sin.

Sin's Corruption of the Family (Gen. 6:1–4)

The family as God gave it and defined it in Genesis 2:24, as being between one man and one woman, was first corrupted by Lamech who decided to take two wives (Gen. 4:19). Here in Genesis 6, the widespread corruption of the family unit by the sons of God, who lusted after the daughters of men and took as many wives for themselves as they could is seen. It is not the point here to identify the sons of God, but rather to observe the far-reaching effects of sin.

FILL IN THE BLANK:

1. Genesis 2:24, "Therefore a _____ shall leave his father and mother and be joined to his _____, and they shall become _____ flesh."

Key Passage

"The earth also was corrupt before God, and the earth was filled with violence. So God looked upon the earth, and indeed it was corrupt; for all flesh had corrupted their way on the earth."

(Gen. 6:11, 12)

In the Beginning — The Creation

POINT: When sin becomes widespread and rampant, women are often devalued and mistreated.

God created woman because it was not good for man to be alone, and she was designed to be man's only suitable companion (Gen. 2:18). In marriage, God designed one man to be bound to one woman where the woman would be understood and treated with honor by her husband (1 Pet. 3:7). This kind of honor is modeled by Jesus in His willingness to love, nurture, and die for the church (see Eph. 5:23–33). Polygamy (a marriage between one man and two or more women) does not follow the original model in Genesis 2:24, where "two become one," and it does not provide the kind of understanding and honor that God intends a wife to receive. Polygamy pits woman against woman in competing for their husband's love. Jacob's wives illustrate this well in Genesis 29 and 30.

FILL IN THE BLANK:

2. Matthew 19:4, 5, "And He answered and said to them, 'Have you not read that He who made them at the beginning 'made them _____ and _____,' and said, 'For this reason a man shall leave his father and mother and be joined to his wife, and the _____ shall become _____ flesh'?"

Sin's Corruption of the Heart (Gen. 6:5–7)

God saw that the wickedness of man was great (Gen. 6:5). God was grieved in His heart for creating man (Gen. 6:6). God said He would destroy man (Gen. 6:7).

God observed the wickedness on the earth.

God called it *great*. It was worldwide; it was everywhere; it covered the whole earth. Everything, good or bad, is seen by God, and nothing can escape His sight.

QUESTION:

3. Do you ever think you have gotten away from doing something you know is wrong? _____
_____

LESSON 8 In the Beginning — Sin and Its Corruption of the World

When God looked upon the earth, it was so rotten with sin that He regretted making man. The Psalmist stated, "The LORD looks down from heaven upon the children of men, To see if there are any who understand, who seek God. They have all turned aside, They have together become corrupt; There is none who does good, No, not one" (Ps. 14:2, 3).

God observed the wickedness in man's heart.

God not only saw what happened on the earth, but He also reads what is in man's heart. God saw not only the thoughts but also that "every intent" (or purpose) of man's thinking was evil continually. Mankind was wicked upon the earth because the heart of man had become obsessed with evil.

QUESTION:

4. What do you suppose Jesus meant when He taught "out of the heart" come many forms of wickedness? _____

_____

"Why did man's heart become so corrupt?"

Paul answers, "And even as they did not like to retain God in their knowledge, God gave them over to a debased mind, to do those things which are not fitting" (Rom. 1:28). They did not like to *retain*, or keep, God in their thinking and planning; He was not kept in their lives; He was not in their daily affairs or pursuits. "The wicked in his proud countenance does not seek God; God is in none of his thoughts" (Ps. 10:4). They had ignored the Governor of the universe and were given over to a debased mind—a mind that was obsessed with evil! When man leaves God, he is left to embrace evil! When he embraces evil, he grows corrupt. However, when we draw closer to Jesus, we renew the spirit of our mind, put off the old corrupt man, and put on a new man (see Eph. 4:20–24).

"What kind of fruit comes from a life that lives away from God?"

Paul asked the Romans this kind of question: "For when you were slaves of sin, you were free in regard to righteousness. What fruit did you have then in the things of which you are now ashamed? For the end of those things is death" (Rom. 6:20, 21).

When people are not following God, they live with self-centered goals. Often such lives are filled with lewd (indecent) conduct and greediness (Eph. 4:19). Lusting, lying, stealing, and using bad language are common traits in living away from God (Eph. 4:19–31). "For we ourselves were also once foolish, disobedient, deceived, serving various lusts and pleasures, living in malice and envy, hateful and hating one another" (Titus 3:3). The ultimate reward for this kind of life is to be repaid with death (Rom. 6:21).

FILL IN THE BLANK:

5. Ephesians 5:6, 7, "Let no one deceive you with empty words, for because of these _____ the _____ of God comes upon the sons of disobedience. Therefore do not be _____ with them."

QUESTIONS:

6. Why was the Lord sorry that He made man (Gen. 6:5)? _____
   _____

7. What is the most deceitful thing according to Jeremiah 17:9? _____
   _____

8. What does it mean to not retain God in our knowledge? _____
   _____

9. Answer the questions from the Scriptures below which show a change that comes in turning to Jesus.

    a. What is in Jesus (Eph. 4:20, 21)? _____
       _____

    b. What is put off (Eph. 4:22)? _____
       _____

    c. What is renewed (Eph. 4:23)? _____
       _____

    d. What is put on (Eph. 4:24)? _____
       _____

LESSON 8 In the Beginning — Sin and Its Corruption of the World

e. What is put away (Eph. 4:25)? _____
_____

f. What are we to do with anger (Eph. 4:26)? _____
_____

g. What does the man, who was a thief, begin doing when he learns Christ (Eph. 4:28)? _____
_____

h. What kind of words come from our mouth as we learn Christ (Eph. 4:29)? _____
_____

i. What are we to put away (Eph. 4:31)? _____
_____

j. How are we to treat others (Eph. 4:32)? _____
_____

Sin's Corruption of Society (Gen. 6:11–13)

A society begins to rot (corrupt) when it moves away from God. Sin is an infection that contaminated the whole world in Noah's day. Its fruit was violence. Think: If man rejects God and His rules, it is only natural for him to also hate and be cruel to his fellow man. If man hates the Creator, why should he love the created? As man travels a path away from God, violence and civil discord arise. This is why God hates those who love violence (Ps. 11:4–7). A *violent* culture is a *rotting* culture.

Because this world became so corrupt and steeped in violence, God counted it worthy for it to be violently destroyed with a flood. We should understand that while God is love, He is incompatible with sin. He cannot tolerate sin. A major message contained in God's word is that He will punish sinners. Adam was condemned for sin and kicked out of the Garden (Gen. 3). Enoch preached against sinners (Jude 1:14, 15). Noah was also a preacher of righteousness and condemned the world in which he had lived (Heb. 11:7).

Living a Righteous Life in a Wicked World (Gen. 6:8, 9)

Genesis 6:8 is set in contrast to what God saw in Genesis 6:5. When God looked at mankind, He saw wickedness on the inside and out.

FILL IN THE BLANK:

10. Genesis 6:5, "Then the LORD _____ that the _____ of _____ was _____ in the earth, and that every intent of the _____ of his _____ was only _____ continually."

11. Genesis 6:8, "But Noah found _____ in the _____ of the LORD."

When God looked at Noah, He saw a just man, a man that He delighted in. Noah was one of the greatest men ever, and like Enoch, he walked with God. With Noah there is a second great message of the Bible: God will forgive and receive those who repent. It was remarkable for Noah to live a righteous life in a climate where acting wicked was the popular thing to do. While the world was racing toward wickedness and doom, Noah was walking with God (believing and obeying Him).

QUESTIONS:

12. Do you ever feel like you are the only one trying to do right?_____
_____
_____
_____

> "By faith Noah, being divinely warned of things not yet seen, moved with godly fear, prepared an ark for the saving of his household, by which he condemned the world and became heir of the righteousness which is according to faith."
>
> (Heb. 11:7)

LESSON 8 In the Beginning — Sin and Its Corruption of the World

By faith Noah worked out his own salvation (Heb. 11:7). Notice:

13. Noah had a faith that *received* the warning. He did not ignore the divine warning, but moved and prepared. God has also warned us through the apostles that a great judgment day of fire is coming (2 Pet. 3:5–13). How will you be like Noah and heed the warning? _____

   _____

   _____

QUESTION:

14. Do you ignore the warnings of your parents at times? Why do you think they warn you about these things? _____

   _____

   _____

   _____

   _____

   _____

Noah had a faith that *feared* the warning. Noah was moved with godly fear. He did not meet it with unbelief, anger, indifference, neglect, or any degree of carelessness as many do today.

Noah had a faith that *obeyed* the warning. Noah was told to build an ark and he obeyed. Genesis 6:22 reads, "Thus Noah did; according to all that God commanded him, so he did." False teachers stress salvation is by *faith alone*. Would Noah have been saved without building the ark? Could Noah build an ark by faith alone? No, he worked obedience by building a gigantic sea vessel which would be about one and a half football fields in length and nearly five stories high! "But do you want to know, O foolish man, that faith without works is dead?" (Jas. 2:20). If Noah and the Ark do not teach salvation by a "faith that works," it teaches *nothing* at all! John, the apostle, stated, "And the world is passing away, and the lust of it; but he who does the will of God abides forever." We must do the will of God to abide.

72   In the Beginning — The Creation

Noah had a faith that *preached* the warning. Noah condemned the world and preached righteousness (2 Pet. 2:5). The judgment of the world was preceded by a warning to the world. This is the way God deals with sinners. He warns them and then destroys them if they do not repent. Many times that warning may be through His followers. Noah was the man for this job, and his faith was not a secret, but one he continuously lived by and preached.

QUESTION:

15. Do you keep your faith a secret? _____

Noah had a faith that inherited the righteousness of faith. That is, God accounted Noah as righteous because he obeyed. He became an heir. When we express our faith in baptism, we also become heirs of God (Gal. 3:26, 27). We are adopted into God's family. Like Noah, we find grace in the eyes of God when we choose to live for Him.

QUESTIONS:

16. How do you think God feels about any violent culture? _____
_____

17. Is it possible to live right in a world that loves wickedness? _____
_____

18. What did Noah find (Gen. 6:8)? _____
_____

19. Must faith have works to be perfect? _____
_____

20. How many people were saved from the flood (1 Pet. 3:20)? _____
_____

21. What has God chosen for man to do to be saved today (1 Pet. 3:21)? ___
_____

LESSON 8 In the Beginning — Sin and Its Corruption of the World

CONCLUSION:

We learn that sin has a tendency to take man further and further away from God. We see that God becomes angry with man's sin, and that sin is worthy of punishment. We also see that no matter how corrupt our world becomes, we always have the ability to resist sin and live for God. God will not allow you to be tempted beyond what you are able to bear (1 Cor. 10:13).

Lesson 9

In the Beginning — Sin's End: Judgment

Genesis 7

How big is sin? The Bible underscores that sin is the basis of man's problems. It brings separation from God, which is spiritual death. It brings a curse to the earth and also to the animals. It brings animosity and hatred between brothers. It brings physical death. It is the ruining agent of every society of men. Genesis 7 further underscores the enormity of sin.

The Bible is the history of sin in Adam's race. The first great message of the Bible is that sin must be punished. It is punished in individuals, in families, in cities, in countries—and here we see it is punished globally! So complete was God's punishment upon sinners that He destroyed *all living* things from the face of the earth (Gen. 7:23). Genesis shows us that sin is incompatible and never agrees with God.

Genesis 7 records a supernatural catastrophe which has never been equaled. Remains of this judgment are found buried in the earth's strata (rock layers). In fact, marine fossils have been found high above the sea level on mountains. This is a testimony to the global flood and God reshaping the earth afterward by making the mountains rise and the ocean valleys sink, as described in Psalm 104:5–9. There is nothing figurative about the Genesis account. It is written in clear, literal language to show us that while God created the world in an open display of amazing power, He is also willing to destroy the world when man chases after sin. It should become very clear to us that God is not concerned with the condition

Key Passage

"For after seven more days I will cause it to rain on the earth forty days and forty nights, and I will destroy from the face of the earth all living things that I have made."

(Gen. 7:4)

of the physical universe, but rather with those He created to inhabit it. Many have become distracted with an artificial concern of global warming. In reality, we should be concerned with the heat of divine anger which is what sin will bring. "Therefore put to death your members which are on the earth: fornication, uncleanness, passion, evil desire, and covetousness, which is idolatry. Because of these things the wrath of God is coming upon the sons of disobedience" (Col. 3:5–6).

The God of the Judgment (Gen. 7:1–5)

Let us notice some things about the God of the judgment of water from Genesis 7:1–5.

> **God is welcoming to the righteous.** He invited Noah, saying, "Come into the ark, you and all your household..." (Gen. 7:1).
>
> **God is discerning.** To be discerning is being able to tell the difference between things. The reason God invited Noah and his family into the ark was because He knew the righteousness of Noah, "...because I have seen that you are righteous before Me in this generation" (Gen. 7:1).
>
> **God is specific.** God gave specific orders to Noah. He did not leave certain things to Noah's own opinion. He commanded Noah to take seven pairs of the clean animals and two of the unclean animals, a male and female. Noah must have understood what God meant by "seven," "two," "clean," "unclean," "male," and "female," as Genesis 7:5 reads, "And Noah did according to all that the LORD commanded him."
>
> **God does not change.** God determined to punish the world in 120 years (Gen. 6:3). Next we find a time stamp of seven days: "For after seven more days I will cause it to rain on the earth forty days and forty nights, and I will destroy from the face of the earth all living things that I have made" (Gen. 7:4). Then we read, "And it came to pass after seven days that the waters of the flood were on the earth" (Gen. 7:10). God doesn't have empty threats. He says what He means and means what He says.

QUESTION:

1. Do your parents ever give you an empty threat? Remember that God does not! Describe an occasion. _____
   _____
   _____

LESSON 9 In the Beginning — Sin's End: Judgment 77

God is severe. God warned that He would destroy man from the face of the earth (Gen. 6:7). He gave the same warning seven days before the flood in Genesis 7:4. Then He did it just as He said: "So He destroyed all living things which were on the face of the ground: both man and cattle, creeping thing and bird of the air. They were destroyed from the earth. Only Noah and those who were with him in the ark remained alive" (Gen. 7:23). (Note: The word for *destroy* in these verses means to *blot* or *scrape away*. It means to wipe something away. Notice how the word is pictured by God in 2 Kings 21:13, "...I will wipe Jerusalem as one wipes a dish, wiping it and turning it upside down." This is what He did when he flooded the world. He *wiped* man off the face of the earth.)

QUESTIONS:

2. How long did it rain on the earth?_____
   _____

3. God could discern or know who was righteous and wicked in Noah's generation. What does God discern between in these verses?

   a. Matthew 13:30 _____
   _____
   _____

   b. Matthew 13:49 _____
   _____
   _____

   c. Matthew 25:1–11 _____
   _____
   _____

   d. Matthew 25:32 _____
   _____
   _____

78 In the Beginning — The Creation

4. As God was specific to Noah about the number, gender, and kinds of animals to bring on the ark, He is also specific today about many things. From the following passages what did God specifically bind? _____

_____

_____

  a. Who and how many did God say could enter into marriage in Mark 10:6–8? _____

  _____

  b. Identify how many things exist from Ephesians 4:4–6. _____

  _____

  _____

5. What did Paul tell the Romans to behold about God in Romans 11:22? __

_____

The Scope of the Judgment (Gen. 7:6–24)

The natural reading of Genesis is that of a worldwide judgment of water. Some today do not want to accept this and try to reduce the magnitude of the flood to a local flood.

QUESTION:

6. Why do men want to pretend it was only a local flood? _____

_____

_____

Perhaps people are disturbed by the small number of people who were saved. Today many want to broaden the scope of who is saved. Some want to believe the ignorant person who never studied about God is saved. Others might say that any "good person" is saved. However, the Genesis flood destroyed the world with an enormous population whereas only eight people were saved. The modern mind who wants to believe that most people are saved finds the teaching of the Genesis flood difficult to accept. Many people think that there are many ways or roads to heaven. They might say "You can go your way with your own beliefs, and I will go my way with my own personal beliefs. In the end, we will all be saved and reach the same goal of heaven." No doctrine defeats "the many roads to heaven" error more thoroughly than the Genesis flood. The New Testament agrees with Genesis by teaching that only eight people in the whole world survived the judgment of water (1 Pet. 3:20). As it was narrow then, so it will be narrow when Jesus comes again (Lk. 13:23–25; Jn. 14:6; 1 Pet. 4:18, 19). Let's identify seven reasons why the flood was global and not a local flood.

FILL IN THE BLANK:

7. 1 Peter 3:20, "who formerly were disobedient, when once the Divine longsuffering waited in the days of Noah, while the ark was being prepared, in which a _____, that is, _____ souls, were _____ through water."

8. Luke 13:24, "Strive to enter through the _____ gate, for _____, I say to you, will seek to enter and will _____ be able."

The size and construction of the ark (Gen. 6:15, 16). Why build such a massive sea vessel to escape a local flood? The ark with three levels has been estimated to have a carrying capacity of 522 standard railroad stock cars. This would equal the ability to carry 125,000 sheep-sized animals! Why build a ship this large if the flood were only regional (Gen. 6:15)? Why not simply escape to another part of the world? If the flood were only local, why not tell Noah what was told to Lot:

> "So He destroyed all living things which were on the face of the ground: both man and cattle, creeping thing and bird of the air. They were destroyed from the earth. Only Noah and those who were with him in the ark remained alive."
>
> (Gen. 7:23)

"Escape to the mountains, lest you be destroyed" (see Gen. 19:17)? We will see below why this advice would prove deadly.

The purpose to keep the species alive (Gen. 7:3). The purpose was to keep the species alive. A local flood would not wipe out the species. Pairs of every kind would come to Noah (Gen. 6:19, 20). This would not require every variation of dog, horse, cattle, ape, etc. that exists today to be taken aboard the ark. It has recently been discovered that wolves are the ancestors of all dogs. So what would have come to Noah? All the genetic material for wolves and dogs today would have existed in that single pair of wolves that came to Noah. Likewise, there are all kinds of variations that we see in man today but all are 100 percent human—all came from Noah's family. God made from one blood every nation of men to dwell on the earth (Acts 17:26). The DNA for all the variation that is seen today (hair color, eyes, tallness, skin, etc.) was present in the life in the ark. All land-dwelling lifeforms that exist today came from those which entered and exited the ark.

The effect of the flood on living creatures (Gen. 7:21–23). The flood destroyed every living creature. No one would ever speak of a local flood as destroying "all living things which were on the face of the earth."

The height of the floodwaters—the mountains were covered (Gen. 7:17–20). Do you see why it would have been deadly for Noah to flee to the mountains? Since water assumes its own level, it cannot be higher than the tallest mountain and be dry anywhere else. No one would speak of a local flood as covering the mountains

The time Noah spent in the ark. Noah went into the ark when he was 600 years, two months, and seventeen days old (Gen. 7:11). He did not come out of the ark until one year and ten days later (Gen. 8:13–16). Why stay in a ship for over a year if it were only a local flood?

The promise to never destroy the earth with a flood (Gen. 9:11).

FILL IN THE BLANK:

9. Genesis 9:11, "Thus I establish My covenant with you: _____ again shall all flesh be cut off by the waters of the flood; _____ again shall there be a _____ to destroy the earth."

Local flood theorists make God out to be a liar and covenant breaker. There have been many devastating local floods throughout man's history on earth. If Noah's flood were a local flood, then Genesis 9:11 is a failed

LESSON 9 In the Beginning — Sin's End: Judgment

promise. However, since it is impossible for God to lie, the flood of Noah must have been global (Heb. 6:18).

The testimony of inspired men.

- The Psalms (Ps. 104:5–9)
- The prophets (Isa. 54:9)
- The apostles (2 Pet. 3:6)
- The Lord (Matt. 24:37–39)—Jesus said the flood came and took them all away. As Noah's flood was global, so Jesus will judge the whole world when He comes again, not a limited area.

QUESTIONS:

10. Read John 3:12. Should we believe God's word when it speaks about earthly things? _____
_____

11. Read John 5:46, 47. Are people to believe Moses' words, or can they choose to not believe his writings and still be acceptable to God? _____
_____
_____

12. Who was saved from the flood, according to Moses? _____
_____

13. How many people did Peter say were saved (1 Pet. 3:20; 2 Pet. 2:5)? ____
_____

14. What did Moses say died in Genesis 7:21? _____
_____

15. Name three reasons why Noah's flood covered the whole world. _____
_____

16. Why did Noah prepare the ark (Heb. 11:7)? _____

_____

_____

_____

CONCLUSION:

We learn many things about God in the judgment against the world by Noah's flood. We should prepare to be saved from a future fiery judgment against the world (2 Pet. 3:7). Peter told us that we can be saved like Noah, through baptism in water and be saved from the judgment of fire that is yet to come (1 Pet. 3:21). The church is God's New Testament ark which Jesus built. We must get into it to be saved by Jesus (Eph. 5:23).

In the Beginning — Noah's Deliverance

Genesis 8

The fossil graveyard in the earth's crust cries out death. Scientists recognize this, and they have phrased an event in the past as *The Great Dying*. This *Great Dying* was a massive die-off of land and marine life in the distant past. Many of these scientists pursue naturalistic explanations. They explain the creation of the universe and the origin of life the same way—a big bang which supposedly exploded out of absolute nothing, which in time supposedly bore life out of non-living material that has evolved over millions of years. These are the kinds of silly ideas which people are left to embrace when they reject the notion of the Creator.

The same silliness is embraced by men who reject the teaching of a global flood. They imagine that there was a mass extinction in the past from a huge asteroid that smashed into the earth. Others imagine that global volcanic activity spewed out enormous amounts of ash into the atmosphere that was destructive to life. Still, others propose that there may have been a spread of toxic water that produced massive land and marine die-offs over thousands or perhaps millions of years. They have little or no evidence to believe these ideas, but they consider them plausible causes. Even if these things did happen, what would have caused them to happen?

Genesis Chapters 6–8 explain the *what*, the *when*, and the *why* for a massive die-off in the past. It was caused because of unrestrained wickedness during the life of Noah that led to a

Key Passage

"Let your conduct be without covetousness; be content with such things as you have. For He Himself has said, 'I will never leave you nor forsake you.'"

(Heb. 13:5)

worldwide judgment of water by the supreme God and Governor of the universe. This position is what best explains the very existence of a fossil record. A gradual die-off over long periods of time would not produce fossils. Fossil preservation requires a rapid burial. This would have happened on a grand scale in the Genesis flood, with the breaking up of the fountains of the deep and the subsequent settling of the sediment. The Bible further explains that during this time, rapid mountain formation occurred (Ps. 104:6–9). God made the valleys sink and the mountains rise. This would explain why we see marine fossils today on mountains thousands of feet above sea level. Likewise, we have the explanation as to why life repopulated on the earth—God remembered Noah and every living thing with him on the ark (Gen. 8:1). Every form of life in the ark had its representation from which it could continue its survival on land.

God Remembered Noah (Gen. 8:1–5)

Genesis 8 continues to show Noah's salvation by grace (Gen. 6:8). It teaches us that God does not forget His people. God does not lose track of those who obey Him. In judgment, God is their refuge and rock. He *remembers,* or *takes note of,* them. God did not forget His people in the terrifying judgments against Egypt. He even made a distinction between their animals and the Egyptians' (Exod. 9:1–7). We are assured in the New Testament that God will not forget our labor; He will not forsake His people (Heb. 6:10; 13:5).

FILL IN THE BLANK:

1. Hebrews 13:5, "Let your conduct be without covetousness; be content with such things as you have. For He Himself has said, 'I will _____ _____ you nor _____ you.'"

QUESTIONS:

2. Name three things God caused to happen when He remembered Noah. _____

_____

3. How many months did the ark float before it rested on a mountain (Gen. 7:11–13 and Gen. 8:4)? _____

_____

4. Where did the ark rest? _____

5. When were the tops of the mountains seen? _____

Noah Waited on God (Gen. 8:6–19)

The reason we read of the month and day of the month should remind us that the things written in Genesis 8 are real history. There are many things we could focus on from this text, but the *patience* of Noah is something to be regarded, especially when we consider the time from which the ark rests until Noah's departure from it. We read "he waited" (Gen. 8:10, 12). When the time is calculated, Noah waited a total of seven months and ten days inside the ark while it was at a standstill on a mountain. We sometimes hear people speak of getting "cabin fever" when they have to be confined indoors after a sickness or surgery. Imagine being confined to a building for over seven months! Waiting on the Lord is being content to not act until there is the command to act from the Lord. Noah had committed himself to doing the commandments of God (Gen. 6:22). It was the Lord who invited Noah to come into the ark (Gen. 7:1). For Noah, it was the Lord who would tell him when to exit the ark. It wasn't until God said, "Go out of the ark," that Noah went.

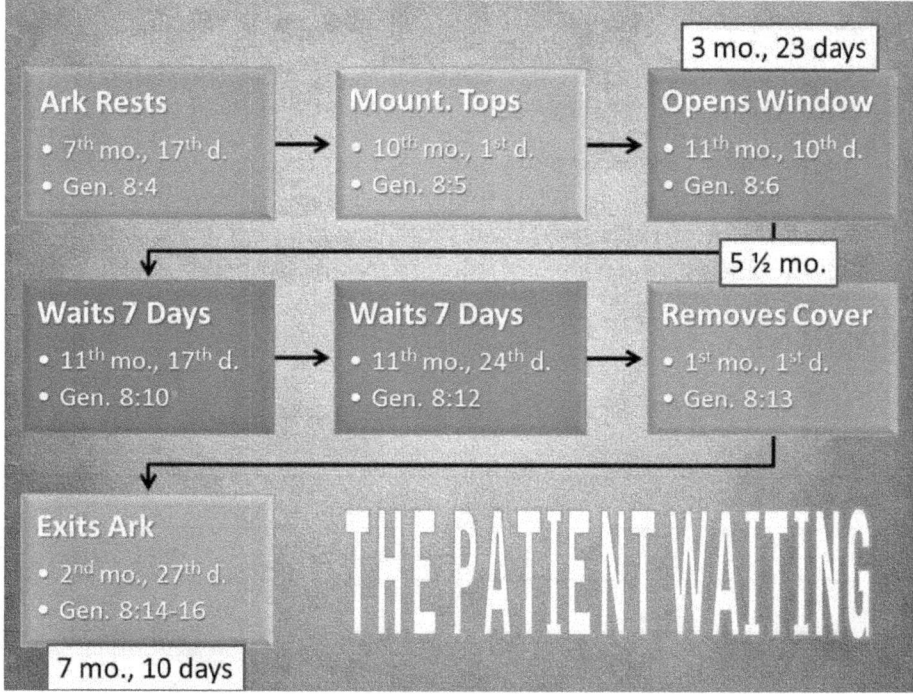

We can learn a lot from Noah, as we are told to wait patiently on the Lord. "Therefore be patient, brethren, until the coming of the Lord. See how the farmer waits for the precious fruit of the earth, waiting patiently until it receives the early and latter rain. You also be patient. Establish your hearts, for the coming of the Lord is at hand" (Jas. 5:7, 8). The farmer has to wait for the fruit of the earth. Its growth is pretty much out of his control. He seeks to provide only the right conditions as much as depends on him to make the fruit come forth. He has to wait on it. Likewise, it is easy for Christians to wonder and grow impatient for the coming of the Lord. We may wonder why the Lord allows the world to continue as our society becomes more and more corrupt. Yet we need to recognize the lesson of Noah. Jesus will not come a second time until the Father commands Him to do so. It is in the Father's time and infinite wisdom to maximize opportunity for those who are being saved. Peter clarified, "The Lord is not slack concerning His promise, as some count slackness, but is longsuffering toward us, not willing that any should perish but that all should come to repentance" (2 Pet. 3:9). Jesus will come as a thief in the night (2 Pet. 3:10). We need to trust Him, wait on Him, and be ready to meet Him.

> *Waiting on the Lord is not always easy.* David penned, "I am weary with my crying; My throat is dry; My eyes fail while I wait for my God" (Ps. 69:3).
>
> *Waiting on the Lord is needed to get through life's trials.* David continued to wait on the Lord in hope even though he was weary. "I wait for the LORD, my soul waits, And in His word I do hope" (Ps. 130:5).
>
> *Waiting on the Lord results in receiving God's goodness.* "The LORD is good to those who wait for Him, To the soul who seeks Him" (Lam. 3:25).
>
> *Waiting on the Lord is needed in bringing others to Christ.* Paul and Silas show this trait in action. While they were unjustly beaten and thrown in prison, they were able to let their light shine brightest by singing hymns (Acts 16:23–25). And it was this that led the other prisoners to listen.

QUESTIONS:

6. What kind of birds did Noah send out of the ark? _____
_____
_____
_____
_____

7. What did the freshly plucked olive leaf tell Noah? _____
   _____
   _____

8. If you were in the ark and knew the ground was dry, would you wait for God to tell you to exit the ark, or would you hastily leave the ark? _____
   _____
   _____

9. Did these people successfully wait on the Lord, or did they react hastily in their circumstances?

    a. Saul (1 Sam. 13:6–11)? _____

    b. David (Ps. 40:1)? _____

    c. Naaman (2 Kin. 5:11, 12)? _____

    d. Israel (Num. 21:4, 5)? _____

    e. The church at Philadelphia (Rev. 3:8)? _____

    f. Jesus (1 Pet. 2:23)? _____

Noah Worshiped God (Gen. 8:20–22)

When Noah stepped off the ark, he stepped into our world. The first recorded action of Noah was the building of an altar and offering a costly sacrifice to the Lord. Noah took one of every clean animal and bird and offered them as a burnt offering to the Lord. This was a sacrifice that showed his profound faith, dependence, and dedication to the Lord. His well-being and even his survival in this new world were in many ways connected to the survival of the animal kingdom. But Noah recognized that God is the sustainer of life and that God would provide for them. Paul said, "for in Him we live and move and have our being…" (Acts 17:28).

88 In the Beginning — The Creation

God received this offering with approval. This is why the Scripture speaks of it as a soothing aroma. It is an expression of divine favor. In Ephesians 5:2, Paul wrote something similar regarding the sacrifice of Christ: "And walk in love, as Christ also has loved us and given Himself for us, an offering and a sacrifice to God for a sweet-smelling aroma." What Jesus did on earth was met with the full approval of the Father. When Paul received preaching support from the church of Christ at Philippi, he described it as a sweet-smelling aroma which he defines as an *acceptable sacrifice, well pleasing to God* (Phil. 4:18).

God made a promise to never destroy the world again with floodwaters. This explains why the world has existed to the present despite man's continued wickedness (Gen. 8:21). But as long as the world exists—that is, until world history ends with the second coming of Christ—seedtime and harvest, the various seasons, and day and night remain.

QUESTIONS:

10. What did Noah offer to God when he exited the ark? _____

_____

_____

11. What does a "soothing aroma" mean? _____

_____

_____

12. Why did God destroy the world? _____

_____

_____

13. Why did God save Noah? _____

_____

_____

14. Will the world last forever or will it eventually be destroyed (2 Pet. 3:10)?

_____

_____

CONCLUSION:

Despite the many observable differences seen today, all human life is traced back to Noah and his wife. The same applies with the animals that were on the ark. While we observe many differences in dogs, it has been discovered that all dogs are actually descendants of wolves. This should help us understand that Noah did not have to bring every breed of dog into the ark but only one pair of wolves. All the variation that is seen today was present within the DNA of the original *wolf couple* that Noah took on the ark.

God is all-powerful and worked an amazing work to save Noah. Noah had a deep and dedicated faith to follow the word of God in building the ark, in entering the ark, and after exiting the ark. Let us have the same kind of faith that Noah had and *move with godly fear* (Heb. 11:7).

Lesson 11

In the Beginning — Life in the New World

The worldwide flood had ended, and Noah and his family had exited the ark, stepping into our present world. As a priest to his family, Noah had offered a large burnt offering unto the Lord. From the aroma of that sacrifice, God promised to never destroy every living thing again as long as the earth remains.

Chapter 9 introduces life in the new world and establishes some principles and general considerations regarding life in it. In this chapter, the covenant God makes with the earth, is given, using the rainbow as the sign of that covenant.

Regulations in the New World (Gen. 9:1–7)

After the terrifying judgment of water, God blessed Noah and his family (Gen. 9:1). When Noah came out of the ark, however, he was given rules to heed.

Reproduce (Gen. 9:1)

FILL IN THE BLANK:

1. Genesis 9:1, "So God blessed Noah and his sons, and said to them: 'Be _____ and _____, and _____ the earth.'"

God restated to Noah what He had said to the first couple (Gen. 1:28). It is interesting that God would want man to multiply knowing how terrible man could become (Gen. 6:5–7). Even more interesting is the fact that God knew

Key Passage

"I set My rainbow in the cloud, and it shall be for the sign of the covenant between Me and the earth." (Gen. 9:13)

"I will never again curse the ground for man's sake, although the imagination of man's heart is evil from his youth; nor will I again destroy every living thing as I have done." (Gen. 8:21)

that man would continue to behave in a corrupt way (Gen. 8:21). Why would God want man to continue to multiply knowing such about man? The answer is simple: God is faithful to every word He says. He still had unfinished promises. He promised that the Seed of woman would give a decisive death blow to the serpent (Gen. 3:15). That had not happened; the scheme of redemption was not yet complete. Though righteous, even Noah and others were still in need of a Savior. God was still working to send His Son to earth to be born of a woman for our redemption (Gal. 4:4, 5).

Reign (Gen. 9:2)

FILL IN THE BLANK:

2. Genesis 9:2, "And the _____ of you and the dread of you shall be on _____ beast of the earth, on _____ bird of the air, on all that move on the earth, and on _____ the fish of the sea. _____ are given into your _____."

Another rule placed on man is for him to reign over the creation. This is similar to what was stated in Genesis 1:26–28. Dominion is restated! Notice the last sentence of verse 2: "They are given into your hand." Every kind of animal is given into the hand of man for him to use for his own benefit and survival. We are told by some people today that animals have rights. If animals do have rights, "Who gives them rights?" If evolution is true, every creature is naturally related to each other. Yet we do not see any animals give out rights. Does a lion in the wilderness give any deer a right? The only rights that we can agree on must come from someone greater than man. Yet, God nowhere gives animals any rights. Who is man to give animals rights when God has not? The reason people reach these silly conclusions is because they have rejected the knowledge and authority of God. Paul identified that foolish thoughts come from foolish hearts which come from a rejection of God. "And even as they did not like to retain God in their knowledge, God gave them over to a debased mind, to do those things which are not fitting" (Rom. 1:28).

The superiority of man over animals is seen in four areas from God's holy word.

- Man was made in God's image (Gen. 1:26–28).

- Man was commissioned to give names to the animals (Gen. 2:19). Do we ever find animals naming man and other creatures?
- The animals are said to have been placed into man's hands and can be consumed without the act of murder being committed (Gen. 9:2–5).
- Man is able to tame animals (Jas. 3:7). He can even tame those animals which have superior strength (Jas. 3:3). Do we ever find animals taming man?

Restriction (Gen. 9:3, 4)

As previously stated, Noah's descendants were now permitted to eat any kind of animal flesh. The relationship of animals to man has changed and is now filled with fear and dread. This is where the *wild* nature begins for animals.

There is an organization called PETA (People for the Ethical Treatment of Animals) that believes it is wrong to eat meat; wear wool, silk, and leather; and attend circuses and zoos. They even believe breeding animals for pets is wrong. The key word to think about is *ethical*. Only people, not animals, can know what is ethical. Without God, however, we would be incapable of knowing what ethical treatment is. Even the founder of PETA has to quote the Lord's golden rule in Matthew 7:12 to define what is *ethical*. However, Jesus applied this rule to *men*, not animals. Animals are incapable of learning or teaching ethics. They hunt and kill each other all the time without thinking about what they have done. They are guided by instinct, not morals. They even prey on their own at times. PETA has no right to use Jesus' rule that was given to men and apply it to animals. Further, the One who gave the golden rule also agreed with Genesis and asked, "... Of how much more value are you than the birds?" (Lk. 12:24; cf. Matt. 6:26). He also asked, "Of how much more value then is a man than a sheep?" (Matt. 12:12). Jesus ate meat and permitted others to do so (Mk. 14:12; Lk. 11:11). Jesus ate fish and honeycomb without thinking how offensive this was to the fish or the bees (Lk. 24:41–43). He chose the apostle Paul to continue to reveal His word (Eph. 3:1–5). Paul taught that all meat can be eaten with prayer and thanksgiving (1 Tim. 4:1–5).

God provided one restriction in eating meat. Man was not to eat meat with the blood. This has always been the case, as the blood was given for atonement for souls (Lev. 17:10–14). The apostles also condemned the eating of blood (Acts 15:28, 29; 21:25).

Reckoning (Gen. 9:5–6)

The Lord transitioned from animal blood to man's bloodshed. When man's lifeblood is shed, God said, "I will demand a reckoning." If an animal kills a man, it is to be put to death. If a man murders a man, he is to be put to death. The reason stated for this law is because a man murdered someone made in the image of God. This law is restated in Exodus 21:12, which is the very next chapter after the Ten Commandments stated, "You shall not murder" (Exod. 20:13). The New Testament also approves capital punishment (Acts 25:11). The government is given the right to bear the sword and avenge evildoers (Rom. 13:1–4).

QUESTIONS:

3. Name the four *R's* given for Genesis 9:1–7. _____
   _____

4. Does God allow man to eat meat? _____

5. What did Jesus eat while on earth? _____

6. What is the "Golden Rule," and was it applied to penguins, peacocks, and parasites or only to people (Matt. 7:24)? _____
   _____
   _____

7. Why was a murderer to be put to death according to Genesis 9:6? ____
   _____

The Covenant & Rainbow (Gen. 9:8–17)

Have you ever seen a rainbow? Do you know why we have rainbows today? What is the significance of a rainbow? Genesis 9 gives us the answer. The rainbow is a sign of the covenant that God made with Noah and the earth. God uses the term *covenant* seven times in this text. This is significant because *seven* means *complete* or *full* in God's word. This covenant will be in place until the world ends. This covenant cannot be altered or taken away as long as the earth remains.

This covenant tells us we now live in the age of forbearance, or mercy. We should see the *longsuffering* as well as the *faithfulness* of God in the rainbow. He is longsuffering because He waits for man to repent; He is faithful because He will not break this covenant regardless of how wicked man is. In fact, three times in the New Testament we read the phrase, "God is faithful" (1 Cor. 1:9; 10:13; 2 Cor. 1:18).

The word *rainbow*, as translated in the New King James Version, is actually the word *bow*. This is the word for the weapon that archers use. God is described in the Scriptures as an archer (Ps. 7:11–13). Hence when He says, "I set My rainbow in the cloud..." (Gen. 9:13), He is saying that He is putting His bow up in the clouds to be a sign. He will not come with vengeance upon the earth, where all flesh is destroyed by floodwaters, again. However, there is a day when there will be no more rainbows, and there will be a judgment of fire. Peter addresses how God once destroyed the world with water, but the heavens and earth which now exist are reserved for a judgment of fire (see 2 Pet. 3:5–10). Sinful man must take advantage of God's mercy now and repent so he can be saved from that day of terror (Acts 17:30, 31).

> "I set My rainbow in the cloud, and it shall be for the sign of the covenant between Me and the earth."
>
> (Gen. 9:13)

FILL IN THE BLANK:

8. Acts 17:30, "Truly, these times of ignorance God _____, but _____ commands _____ men everywhere to _____."

Sin in the New World (Gen. 9:18–29)

The world was repopulated by Noah's sons and their wives (9:18, 19). However, there is the same problem in this world that existed in the previous world—sin! Man can be tempted and drawn away to do evil here.

96 In the Beginning — The Creation

FILL IN THE BLANK:

9. James 1:14, "But _____ one is _____ when _____ is drawn away by his _____ _____ and enticed."

Even though Noah was a righteous man who stood against sin, he fell into sin here. The Bible shows the weakness of its heroes. There is only one Man who never sinned, and He is the Son of God. Noah became a farmer and vinedresser. There was nothing wrong with this. Grapes are in fact a blessing given to man for eating and drinking. (1 Sam. 25:18; Isa. 65:8). However, when the juice becomes fermented (which is a decaying process), the blessing is turned into a curse for a man if he drinks it. "New wine," or unfermented wine, is spoken of as a blessing in Proverbs 3:9, 10. However, when it becomes fermented and intoxicating, it is condemned without reservation as being addicting, obscuring the senses, and in general making a mockery of man (Prov. 20:1; 23:29–35; 31:4, 5).

Noah's sin led to another sin. In his drunken stupor, Noah became undressed, and his son Ham came into the tent and began to gaze at his father's nakedness (Gen. 9:22). Ham went out and told his brothers and likely acted disrespectfully toward Noah. Shem and Japheth walked backward into the tent not looking upon their father and covered him.

QUESTIONS:

10. What do you think of when you see a rainbow? _____

    _____

11. Where did God set His rainbow? _____

    _____

12. Fill in the blanks, "Wine is a _____, Strong drink is a _____, And whoever is led astray by it is not _____" (see Proverbs 20:1).

13. In Proverbs 23:29–35, who did Solomon say will have woe, sorrow, contentions, complaints, and wounds? _____

    _____

    _____

Both Old and New Testaments show sin to be man's problem. Our sins are what took Jesus to the cross so that we might have forgiveness if we obey His will. Only in His cross can we find our sins forgiven, and only in baptism can we contact that saving death (Rom. 6:3, 4). Though Noah lived 950 years, he still died (Gen. 9:28, 29). Death is common for all. Ethan the Ezrahite asked, "What man can live and not see death? ..." (Ps. 89:48). The New Testament teaches that it is appointed for men to die once and then the judgment (Heb. 9:27). Let us prepare for that judgment by being saved by the blood of Jesus Christ.

In the Beginning — The Beginning of Languages and Nation Formation

The Bible is filled with the history of man. Many people enjoy reading about their personal history and discovering who lived in their family tree. Sometimes they discover a very famous person is in their family tree. Perhaps they take pride in that fact, but such really adds nothing to our character or standing with God.

The Jews thought they could be accepted because Abraham was their father. John the baptizer told them, "Therefore bear fruits worthy of repentance, and do not begin to say to yourselves, 'We have Abraham as our father.' For I say to you that God is able to raise up children to Abraham from these stones" (Lk. 4:8). As for having a very famous person in our genealogy, we all have Noah. Simply because we are from the lineage of Noah doesn't mean that we are acceptable with God. Paul taught that we can become children of God and have Jesus and Abraham in our genealogy when we by faith, are baptized into Christ (Gal. 3:26–29).

Genesis Chapter 10 gives us our family tree, as every one of us is from Noah through one of his three sons: Shem, Ham, or Japheth. We can all say, "I survived the flood!" because we did through Noah and his family. Genesis chapter 10 is critically important because it gives us a table of nations. "These were the families of the sons of Noah, according to their generations, *in their nations*; and from these, the nations were divided on the earth after the flood" (Gen. 10:32, emp. added). The building of these nations and their identity took place after the tower of Babel that is described in Genesis Chapter 11.

Key Passage

"And He has made from one blood every nation of men to dwell on all the face of the earth, and has determined their preappointed times and the boundaries of their dwellings."

(Acts 17:26)

Japheth's Decendants—Read Genesis 10:1-5

The nations of Noah's sons have some names which are difficult to determine and others which seem easier. Recall that Japheth was spoken of as being "enlarged" (Gen. 9:27). It seems that his descendants excelled in exploration and became extensive in their occupancy of great portions of the world. His descendants became nations in Europe, eastward in northern Iran, and likely some migrated through Russia and perhaps down through the Bearing Strait into the Americas. A Jewish man living in the first century named Josephus identified Gomer as the founder of the Galatians in his book *The Antiquities of the Jews*.[1] He also identified Magog as the founder of the Scythians; Madia as the Medes who were in the northern portion of modern-day Iran. Javan seems to be the founder of Greece, as this word is translated in Daniel 8:21. Ashkenaz has been identified by some for Germany. Togarmah is the ancestor of the Armenians. Tarshish has been connected to Tartessos in southern Spain. When you look at a map, you can see that Japheth became very large by migrating throughout the world.

Ham's Decendants—Read Genesis 10:6-20

From Ham, we find that his descendants moved down in Africa and east of the Mediterranean Sea. His eldest son, Cush, is evidently the father of the Ethiopians. This word is translated as *Ethiopia* in Esther 1:1 and many other places. Cush had a son named Nimrod who began the first kingdom of the Bible, and he reigned over a large area in the Mesopotamian valley, much of what is present-day Iraq. He began to be mighty on the earth as well as being a powerful hunter. Significantly, the beginning of his kingdom was Babel, which is where man became divided into nations by God confusing their languages (Gen. 11). Ham's second born, Mizraim, is the name for Egypt. The Scripture also shows the Philistines had their ancestry in him. Ham's third son, Put, is seemingly the ancestor of Libya and is translated as such in Ezekiel 27:10. There, they were in an alliance with the nations of Tyre, Persia, and Lydia. Canaan, the fourth son of Ham, is the ancestor of several nations east of the Mediterranean Sea, whom Israel would frequently battle.

---

[1] Antiq. 1.6.1.

LESSON 12 In the Beginning — The Beginning of Languages and Nation Formation

Shem's Decendants—Read Genesis 10:20-31

This brings us to the nations from Shem. Shem is mentioned last because he has a very significant role: Through him, the Seed of promise would come to bring heaven's blessings of redemption for all families of the earth. Josephus explains that the Persians came from Elam, the Assyrians came from Asshur and settled in Nineveh, and the Chaldeans (Babylonians) came from Arphaxad. The significant point of interest about Arphaxad is that he is an ancestor of "Eber" who is an ancestor of Abram the "Hebrew" (Gen. 14:13). The word *Hebrew* came from the word *Eber* and means "one from beyond." So by following the genealogies of Chapters 10 and 11, we trace the lineage from Noah down to Abraham who is called the *Hebrew*, through whom significant promises were made.

QUESTIONS:

1. From which son of Noah did the Europeans come? _____

   _____

2. Where did most of Ham's descendants choose to live? _____

   _____

3. Where did Nimrod begin his kingdom? _____

   _____

4. Why did Eber name his son Peleg (Gen. 10:25)? _____

   _____

5. How many years passed after the flood when Arphaxad was born (Gen. 11:10)? _____

   _____

6. The lifespans for those who lived after the flood shrank from those who lived before the flood. What is the total number of years that Arphaxad lived (Gen. 11:12, 13)? _____

   _____

7. Who was Abram's father, and how many years did he live (Gen. 11:27, 32)?

   _____

8. Which son of Noah do you think you are related to? _____

   _____

The Tower of Babel (Gen. 11:1–9)

God had commanded Noah and his family to "Be fruitful and multiply, and fill the earth" (Gen. 9:1). However, exploring the earth had stalled out on a plain in the land of Shinar. Man ceased to journey and began to construct a city with a massive tower. God is not opposed to big buildings or to cities; He is opposed to rebellion and pride. Man's ambitious goal was to build a tower whose top would be in the heavens. Their motive was two-fold. They wanted to make a name for themselves, and they did not want to be *scattered* over the face of the whole earth (Gen. 11:4). This motive runs directly opposite to the Lord's command to *fill* the earth. It was a willful act of rebellion. Likely Nimrod, whose name means "rebellion," was a leader of this, as he began his kingdom at Babel (Gen. 10:10). He had impressed men with his ability to hunt animals and gained respect to build an empire. This work glorified human achievement and rebelled against the Creator of the earth. Rather than living in tents to be moved about and explore the world, their opposition was further seen in the burning clay to make immovable bricks to build their city. It is likely from this event that many of the religions, beliefs of various gods (polytheism), and the worship of heavenly bodies were born. Paul taught that God's attributes had been clearly seen from the beginning of creation and that man, even though he knew God, chose not to glorify Him and changed His glory into an image of man, beast, bird, etc. (Rom. 1:18–23).

Any society that is man-centered and not God-centered is destined to failure. Whenever man resists God, he will ultimately and always be defeated. The Psalmist penned, "Why do the nations rage, And the people plot a vain thing? The kings of the earth set themselves, And the rulers take counsel together, Against the LORD and against His Anointed, saying, 'Let us break Their bonds in pieces And cast away Their cords from us.' He who sits in the heavens shall laugh; The Lord shall hold them in derision" (Ps. 2:1–4).

God came down to see the works of man (Gen. 11:5). God is interested in what we do, and He is watchful over man's works and heart.

LESSON 12 In the Beginning — The Beginning of Languages and Nation Formation

FILL IN THE BLANK:

9. Genesis 6:5, "Then the LORD _____ that the wickedness of man was great in the earth, and that every intent of the thoughts of his _____ was only evil continually."

"The LORD is in His holy temple, The LORD'S throne is in heaven; His eyes behold, His eyelids test the sons of men" (Ps. 11:4). The Lord saw that man was unified and had disobeyed God's rule to fill the earth. By a divine act the Lord confused their speech, giving them different languages. Before Babel, man spoke one language; here we find the origin of all the various languages in the world.

Language is an amazing component of being made in the image of God. Only humans can communicate their will, emotions, concepts, and ideas to each other by clear and concise words. Language allows man to be very precise. Language is not something that evolved over time, but rather, it is something that God gave man. We previously saw that Adam, the first man, was able to name all the animals that walked before him (Gen. 2:19). Adam even named his wife, Eve, because she is the mother of all living (Gen. 3:20). They named their children with names that had meaning. Cain means *possession*, Abel means *breath*, and Seth means *compensation*. In naming Seth, Eve believed God was *compensating*, *repaying* or *providing*, her another son for the murder of Abel. Words are vessels of information! Since man is a highly intelligent creature capable of understanding complex ideas and debating issues, it only makes sense that he would have ways to communicate information in a clear way. The teaching from Genesis 11:1–9 shows us:

> "There are, it may be, so many kinds of languages in the world, and none of them is without significance."
>
> (1 Cor. 14:10)

- That the root of all languages is from God, not evolution.
- That early man was intelligent and capable of building very large structures.
- How powerful unity is.
- That God takes interest in the works of man.
- That God can disapprove and defeat the works of man.
- That building large buildings does not make us great in the eyes of the Lord.
- The key for understanding the variations that exist in people today.

About 100 years after Noah got off the ark, God created distinct languages, confused man, and upset his tower project. Those families which could speak the same language would have gathered together to form people groups. This would cause them to migrate away, or be divided into people groups. This would have resulted in the isolation of the DNA pool in each group where various observational differences would have presented (skin color, eyes, stature, etc.). These people groups would eventually become nations, and the languages which they had would continue to change over time. For an example of this, find a King James Version of the Bible, and notice how the English language was in the year A.D. 1611. It is very different from the way language is spoken today.

TRUE OR FALSE:

- T or F   God opposes man building large structures.
- T or F   God does not like cities.
- T or F   God confused the languages of man because they rebelled against God's command to fill the earth.
- T or F   Language has evolved over millions of years from grunts and groans to a highly technical and precise form of communication.
- T or F   God is the author of all languages.
- T or F   Nimrod was a powerful hunter.
- T or F   You are a descendant of Noah.

LESSON 12 In the Beginning — The Beginning of Languages and Nation Formation

Genesis Chapters 10 and 11 are not filled with useless information. These chapters connect all people to the history of the flood and Noah's family. There is special information that connects Noah to Abraham in whom God would continue to fulfill His promise to bring forth the Messiah for our redemption.

In the Beginning — The Beginning of the Scheme of Redemption

Chapters 10 and 11 take us from Shem and introduce us to Abram, the son of Terah (Gen. 11:26). Abram is mentioned as having two brothers, Nahor and Haran. Abram was a native of Ur of the Chaldeans and was married to Sarai. In Ur, he was called to leave his country and go to a land that God would show him. The New Testament reveals that he had no idea where he was going: "By faith Abraham obeyed when he was called to go out to the place which he would receive as an inheritance. And he went out, not knowing where he was going" (Heb. 11:8). Nevertheless, Abram obeyed God by faith.

Genesis 12:1–3 is a very important passage of Scripture which reveals three central promises that the rest of the Bible brings to fulfillment. It begins to bring about the solution to the big problem of sin. Where sin brought *curses*, the promise to Abram speaks of *blessings*. From this text the theme of the Bible is known. It is the redemption of man from sin, through Jesus Christ. As you read the remainder of the Bible, ask yourself, "How does this relate to the promise to Abraham?" Let's look at the text carefully.

The Land Promise (Gen. 12:1)

God was going to lead Abram to a land that He would show him. In Genesis 12:5–7, Abram, with Sarai and Lot (Abram's nephew), left Haran and began to head toward "the land of Canaan." This is the land where the descendants of Ham's son, Canaan, had migrated after the tower of Babel. It went from Sidon down through Gaza and

Key Passage

"Now the LORD had said to Abram: "Get out of your country, from your family and from your father's house, to a land that I will show you. I will make you a great nation; I will bless you and make your name great; and you shall be a blessing. I will bless those who bless you, and I will curse him who curses you; and in you all the families of the earth shall be blessed."

(Gen. 12:1–3)

over toward Sodom and Gomorrah (see Gen. 10:15-19). After Abram had passed through the land, the Lord appeared to him and said, "To your descendants I will give this land" (Gen. 12:7). The familiar phrase, "Promised Land," comes from this passage. God had promised Abram that he would give the land of Canaan to his descendants. This very promise would be fulfilled hundreds of years later through Joshua's conquest: "So the LORD gave to Israel all the land of which He had sworn to give to their fathers, and they took possession of it and dwelt in it" (Josh. 21:43). In fact, not a word failed (Josh. 21:45). God keeps His promises!

> "Not a word failed of any good thing which the LORD had spoken to the house of Israel. All came to pass."
>
> (Josh. 21:45)

QUESTIONS:

1. Did Abraham know where he was going when the Lord called him to leave his country? _____
   _____

2. Would you like to pack up all your belongings and move to another country without even knowing your destination? _____
   _____

3. What land is the "promised land"? _____
   _____

4. Did God keep His word in giving Abraham's descendants the Promised Land? _____
   _____

5. Read Psalm 44:1-3. By whose strength was Israel able to take the Promised Land? _____
   _____
   _____

6. Using a New King James Version, fill in the blanks of what Solomon said: "Blessed be the LORD, who has given rest to His people Israel, according to all that He _____. There has not _____ one _____ of all His good _____, which He _____ through His servant Moses" (1 Kin. 8:56).

The Nation Promise (Gen. 12:2)

A second primary promise to Abraham was that God would make a nation out of Abraham's descendants. This would take hundreds of years to be fulfilled. God explained to Abraham that his descendants would become strangers in another land and be reduced to servants of that nation (Gen. 15:13). But God would judge that nation and bring them out from it with great possessions. This would begin to be fulfilled through the life of Joseph and eventually be completed hundreds of years later by Moses. It states in Exodus 12:35, 36, "Now the children of Israel had done according to the word of Moses, and they had asked from the Egyptians articles of silver, articles of gold, and clothing. And the LORD had given the people favor in the sight of the Egyptians, so that they granted them what they requested. Thus they plundered the Egyptians."

The Seed Promise (Gen. 12:3)

The third and most significant promise made to Abraham was regarding his Seed. God told Abraham that "...in you all the families of the earth shall be blessed" (Gen. 12:3). God was doing this special work in Abraham, and it would result in a blessing by which all the families of the earth would be blessed. It was not only one nation, but every single family in every single nation. As sin is universal, so the blessing through Abraham is extended to everyone. What did God mean when He said "in you"? After Abraham was tested by God in offering up his son Isaac, God further explained this promise, saying, "In your seed all the nations of the earth shall be blessed, because you have obeyed My voice" (Gen. 22:18).

The blessing for all nations would be in Abraham's seed. This promise was fulfilled in Jesus Christ. Paul wrote, "But when the fullness of the time had come, God sent forth His Son, born of a woman, born under the law, to redeem those who were under the law, that we might receive the adoption as sons" (Gal. 4:4, 5). Just before this Paul penned, "For as many of you as were baptized into Christ have put on Christ," and, "And if you are Christ's, then you are Abraham's seed, and heirs according to the promise" (Gal. 3:27, 28). Anyone who obeys the gospel becomes an heir of the promise

110 In the Beginning — The Creation

to Abraham, because in doing so, he becomes Abraham's seed. How does he become the offspring of Abraham? It is by being baptized into Christ that we reach these promises. Jesus Christ is the "Seed" of Abraham, as Paul revealed by the Holy Spirit, "Now to Abraham and his Seed were the promises made. He does not say, 'And to seeds,' as of many, but as of one, 'And to your Seed,' who is Christ" (Gal. 3:16).

QUESTIONS:

7. Name the three key promises to Abraham in Genesis 12:1–3. _____
   _____
   _____
   _____

8. When did Abraham become a "great nation"? _____

9. Who is the Seed of Abraham that is spoken of in Scripture? _____
   _____

10. How can we become partakers of the blessings of Abraham today? ____
    _____
    _____

11. What did God promise:

    a. Before time began (Titus 1:2)? _____
       _____

    b. To one who wants to do God's will (Jn. 7:17)? _____
       _____

    c. To one who keeps God's word (Jn. 14:23)? _____
       _____

LESSON 13 In the Beginning — The Beginning of the Scheme of Redemption

    d. To one who repents and is converted to Christ (Acts 3:19)? _____

_____

    e. To one who loves Him (Jas. 2:5)? _____

_____

    f. To one who is tempted (1 Cor. 10:13)? _____

_____

    g. To those who will go to heaven (Rev. 21:4)? _____

_____

CONCLUSION:

All the rest of the Bible is about fulfilling the promise God made to Abraham in Genesis 12:1–3. It is very important for us to know this Scripture and the promises made by God. It is also extremely important to discover the Seed of Abraham and have the same kind of faith Abraham had in obeying the Lord, so that we can be blessed with Abraham and have the redemption of our souls by the blood of Jesus Christ

www.ingramcontent.com/pod-product-compliance
Lightning Source LLC
Chambersburg PA
CBHW070449050426
42451CB00015B/3414